MYSTERIES OF THE MERSEY VALLEY

Peter Hough and Jenny Randles

SIGMA Leisure

Published by Sigma Leisure – an imprint of
Sigma Press, 1 South Oak Lane, Wilmslow, Cheshire SK9 6AR, England.

British Library Cataloguing in Publication Data
A CIP record for this book is available from the British Library.

ISBN: 1-85058-355-2

Typesetting and Design by: Sigma Press, Wilmslow, Cheshire.

Cover illustration: Jay Hurst

Printed by: Manchester Free Press

General Disclaimer

Whilst every effort has been made to ensure that the information given in this book is correct, neither the publisher nor the authors accept any responsibility for any inaccuracy.

Preface

Welcome to *Mysteries of the Mersey Valley*. The River Mersey with its genesis in Stockport, meanders through forty miles of urban conurbations and Cheshire countryside before releasing its life force into the Irish Sea at Liverpool. On its way the river skirts Manchester, feeds the famous Ship Canal, flows through Warrington then broadens into an estuary rich in wildlife, and adversely, pollution generating heavy industry.

The river is more than a geographical feature. It is a cultural focus for stories, legends and modern mysteries. The Mersey is a silver thread that weaves through the invisible world of the paranormal and the supernatural. A world that occasionally interacts with our own bringing forth a magic both light and dark, and utterly bewildering.

We have traced the river's magical legacy down countless centuries. Ironically we have used two man-made boundaries for the limits of our Valley. They are the A580 (East Lancashire Road) to the north, and the M56 to the south. Between these perimeters we have uncovered a dazzling array of stories concerning ghosts, witchcraft, corn circles, dragons, aliens, mermaids, poltergeist phenomena, UFO encounters and other anomalies.

As full-time writers and researchers into the Unexplained, many of the modern cases are the results of our own personal investigations. Places, dates and names are given, but note that names of witnesses denoted with an asterisk (*) have been changed to ensure anonymity; all others are actual names of those who witnessed the event described.

This present work follows the Mersey Valley through eight sections. Each section is headed with a map which pin points the locations of the various phenomena, so you can visit the places yourself. If you wish to delve beyond the surface narrative we advise you to seek out our other books, some of which are listed at the back of this one.

Please read on, and enjoy, but remember – next time it could happen to you!

Jenny Randles and Peter Hough

ACKNOWLEDGEMENTS

We would like to thank the following individuals who have assisted us: Danny Cheveaux, Brian Fishwick, Mark Glover, Andy Roberts, Peter Rogerson, Roy Sandbach and the staff of BUFORA, Arthur Tomlinson, Granada TV, Jodrell Bank Science Centre, Leigh Library, Mersey Television ('Brookside') and Radio City.

CONTENTS

1

MERSEY SOURCERY

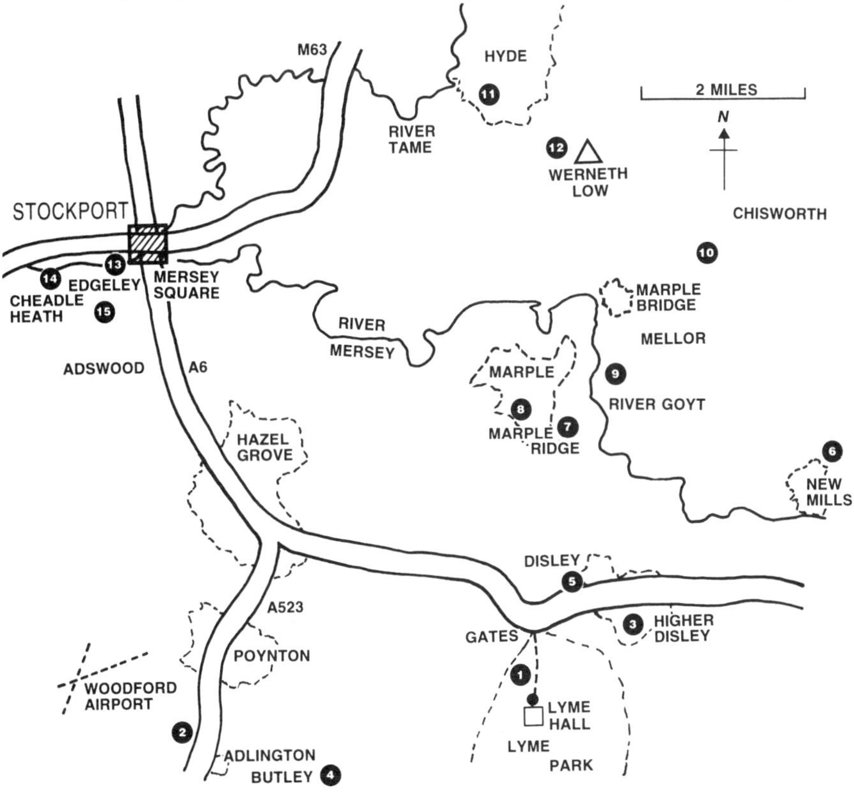

1. Lyme Park Ghost
2. Adlington Computer Poltergeist
3. Higher Disley Lights
4. Butley UFO
5. Disley Lights
6. New Mills Phantom Cat
7. Marple Ridge Crop Circle
8. Marple UFO
9. Bottoms Hall UFO
10. Brown Low Car Stop
11. Hyde Poltergeist
12. Werneth Low Mystery Cloud
13. Castle Street 'Ley'
14. Cheadle Heath UFO
15. Adswood Flying Camera

The Pennine springs, Stockport and North-east Cheshire

The River Mersey is born amid rain-swept millstone grit beneath the bleak and oddly beautiful Pennine moors. The hills brood over sprawling conurbations of industrial Lancashire fending off all but the hardiest of invaders from Yorkshire to the east.

Tributary streams, the Goyt and Tame, flow respectfully south through Tameside and north from the Derbyshire peaks around New Mills. In Stockport town centre, they merge to become the slumbering Mersey, which starts a winding 40-mile trek towards the sea across the lush flood plains that link Manchester with Liverpool.

The river itself begins out of sight, underneath an area paved by armies of marching feet and fleets of supermarket trolleys. One of the north-west's busiest shopping centres has been concreted over the waterway and named, quite naturally, Mersey Square. Here Europe's largest brick-built structure, the newly refurbished viaduct, strides majestically across the fledgling river and affords rail travellers who are passing through a panoramic view of the route to either side.

Thus is born a river whose flow from east to west divides prosperous Cheshire to its south from hard-working Lancashire in the north. In 1974 the faceless planners then saw fit to discard history and invent hypothetical counties, Greater Manchester and Merseyside, hoping that they might rein in the river's two extremities. Few locals adhere to their dismal plan.

In this first part of the book we will look at some of the mysteries and unexplained phenomena that surround the region where Tame and Goyt unite amid the sandstone gorge of Stockport. As the commercial heart of north-east Cheshire this hosts many a strange tale, and set us up nicely for the riddles we shall confront on the journey west towards the sea.

The Lyme Park spooks

Lyme Hall is a popular attraction on the A6 east of Stockport centre, half a mile before Disley village is reached. It is open to the public and surrounded by parkland with a much loved herd of deer. It is also heavily shrouded in history. So reflective of English heritage is the land that even the Australian soap opera *Neighbours* filmed scenes here when it needed to present that sedate and sombre image of the aristocrat.

Records show that a building stood on the site in the fifteenth century and the Legh family has lived there for over 500 years. The present building was redesigned in 1720 but its ghosts hark back to much earlier days.

The most famous Lyme ghost is the funeral procession, said to be witnessed on well moonlit but cloudy nights, marching slowly and silently across the grounds. Among its number is a woman in white, who contrasts with the other members of the cortege. Legend has it that she is Blanche, an unrequited lover of Sir Piers Legh II whose funeral appears to be replayed around the slight hill between entrance and hall.

Legh was a knight who saved the king at Agincourt in 1415. He did so by way of a brilliant tactical manoeuvre against the French. But he paid with his own life. The wounds were lingering and when he did succumb in 1422 it was his last wish that he brought home to Stockport to be buried.

Blanche reputedly never recovered from the sight of Piers funeral and killed herself by the banks of the nearby River Bollin. Her white spectral form has been seen on a number of occasions in the Long Gallery; although more often the reports speak only of a sobbing, moaning sound from the room.

There is another phantom associated with what is locally known as the Ghost Room; although this is also supposedly a place where Mary Queen of Scots was temporarily incarcerated. But the apparition here would seem not to be Mary herself. Instead, it is thought to be a man whose skeleton was excavated from a small hiding hole underneath the floorboards.

It would seem that this man had been imprisoned in this tiny, dark space and left to die slowly through starvation. The terrible emotion that must have filled the air in those final agonising hours may have left a lasting imprint like a signal on a video tape, to be screened before unwitting visitors who chance to be in the wrong place at the wrong moment.

The ghost in the machine

Ghosts, like most things, seem to move with the times. Just a mile west of Lyme Park is Poynton. It was here in 1988 that some odd things were going on in a new hi-tech factory on the Adlington road. One of their computers was reputedly taken over by a poltergeist.

Despite not being switched on at the time, the VDU (visual display unit) would burst into life for no apparent reason. It was as if an unseen force had taken hold of it and charged up the screen into an eerie glow.

These phantom happenings often occurred in the middle of the night. The power socket was disconnected, yet somehow the screen still began to operate. It got so bad that experts were called in from the computer manufacturers. They were as perplexed as anybody.

One idea that was mooted was that leaking energy from the radar systems at Woodford Airport might be to blame. Woodford was close to the factory and, as a base where military aircraft were built and flown, tended to be quite active with technological wizardry. Could some beam that they were accidentally emitting perhaps fill the wires with life?

However, even if radiation leaking from the radar could have charged the screens, this theory seems doomed as a solution to the case. Operating times were checked and the radar was switched off during the periods when the ghost took over the machine.

In the end it was decided to replace the computer with another and it seems that the apparitions ceased when this was done. But the problem of computer jinxes has become increasingly common. It is known that some people can affect modern household equipment just by passing near them. Certain office workers cause all manner of things to go wrong because of electrical fields that are found inside all of our bodies.

Jacqueline Priestman, a Stockport woman, suffered when her vacuum cleaners kept blowing up through sudden power surges. Replacing them made no difference. Then her iron burst into flames. Dr Michael Shallis, an Oxford research scientist, found she had many times the normal static charge within her system. This only subsided when Mrs Priestman chanced to alter her diet.

In the past we have interpreted this very natural energy eruption as an infestation of evil spirits. In truth it seems to be more mundane – simply an illustration that at times all our bodies can be shocking.

The Disley lights

Lyme Park is also haunted by those contemporary space-age ghosts – strange lights in the sky.

On 1 May 1990 Jodrell Bank, who pass onto us sightings of odd goings on around the north-west, channelled a report from two youths at Higher Disley who were looking south west towards Bowstones gate.

An arc of red light illuminated the horizon forming a solid dome. It resembled a rounded triangle but as the lights within this apparition fell towards the ground the dome flattened out into a red line speckled with twinkling dots. These then slowly fell behind the Bowstones hill range, whose summit glowed yellow as if aflame with misty light.

It seems unlikely these were lights from either Manchester or Woodford Airport; although the weather conditions did suggest that a mirage might have formed and this could have been bending car headlights into the sky to produce a spectral aura.

The result would have been akin to an oasis seen in a desert, or those puddles that mysteriously appear on the road ahead when driving on a hot summer's day. Both bodies of water are illusions, just patches of blue sky whose light rays have been bent so that they appear on the ground. In reverse, ground lights can also be projected into the sky to form UFOs.

However, Lyme Park has had more than its fair share of strange lights. A classic encounter, at Butley, just south of Adlington, took place in broad daylight and is very difficult to explain in normal terms.

It occurred outside a local inn, the Ash Tree, a location for stories of hauntings in a more traditional sense. Footsteps from an unseen source have been heard and there is a 'creepy spot', as it was described, where some customers claim to sense a feeling of discomfort. A toby jug has also been reported to move across a room of its own devices, until it was taken from the building and has acted normally ever since.

Apart from these stories, the pub is a warm, friendly place much loved by the locals, and the rather infrequent visitations by the ghost seem not to deter anyone from enjoying its undoubted delights.

The extra-terrestrial phantom that visited Butley village did so on 16 September 1981 and made its mark right outside the Ash Tree.

At 8am on that morning, villager Roy Walton* was walking his dog on the Bollington Road when a disc-like object appeared low in the sky to the west. It moved very slowly towards the power lines, halting directly above them only a few feet in the air.

The object was an oval with a flat base ringed by curved windows that were shaped like the insets in a beer glass. A dark pole emerged from the side of the object with a small box on the end. This slowly rotated (anti-clockwise as seen from below) as if scanning or, indeed, sucking up energy from the power lines.

As the witness was taking all of this in a young man arrived on a bicycle and nearly fell off his saddle in astonishment; traffic was moving past on the A523 as if utterly oblivious to the invader.

After about two minutes, the arm on the object stopped rotating and it moved eastward towards Bollington, before hovering over more power lines and returning back in an arc towards Alderley Edge.

That night in the pub the locals discussed the strange intruder. Several regulars were airline pilots based at Manchester Airport and one was determined to prove that it was merely a rogue weather balloon. But he enquired next day and found that there were none in the area. Indeed nobody knew what this peculiar object was.

Still the incidents surrounding Lyme Park continue. At 8.30 on the evening of 4 March 1992 a woman in her twenties was walking her dog in Disley just a few hundred yards north of the park gates when the animal looked skyward, attracted by something that to her owner was silent. Following the creatures gaze the woman spotted a huge glowing doughnut ringed with round lights or windows. The object almost seemed to be smiling!

The glowing mass moved at speed in a smooth and very rapid course from the south to the north, first appearing directly over the hill where the ghostly funeral procession is said to occur and disappearing suddenly above a golf course and disused quarry towards the River Goyt. A small red light, hugging the ground contours like the giant object had done, zipped past in its wake and was lost over the horizon.

The relationship between these strange lights and outcrops or quarries is well established. Some researchers think they are a product of stresses within the quartz crystal structure of these rocks. The name 'earthlights' has been coined to describe such age-old phenomena.

Mysterious moggies

Just north of Lyme Park, on the Goyt itself, is New Mills, a steeply inclined town forged from the local rock. It has quite a tradition of strange phenomena, including dazzling light shows that parade across the hills to both the south and to the west near Strines.

But its most curious feature is the appearance of the mysterious big cat that stalks the local hillsides.

Britain has no native animals akin to the ferocious puma, panther or lynx, yet there are persistent reports that these are being seen – particularly in Exmoor where both army and cryptozoologists (hunters of out of place creatures) combined but failed to capture an example. However, the New Mills panther is a rare critter being seen in the north.

Reports began about 1982 in the farmland surrounding New Mills and Hayfield, just to its west. In 1988 a farmer at Weathercotes even alleged that it might have been responsible for the terrible injuries suffered by some of his lambs, found with bite marks alongside strange animal paw prints within the field.

In November 1989 Steve Monaghan of a New Mills farm took one very blurred distant photograph of a black panther and a local policeman also saw it resting on a rock as if sun bathing. The Ollersett Moor region was stalked by marksman for several days. They were issued a 'shoot to kill' order, fearing that if tranquillised the animal might cause considerable harm until the drug took effect. But the phantom cat disappeared into the moors just as quickly as it had appeared.

Some experts thought that the image just about detectable on the photograph could perhaps be a wild dog or large feral (wild) cat. The witnesses were adamant it was not. Two years later the reports began again. A black cat said to be a panther was seen on Laneside Road in New Mills.

Mrs Kathleen Topliff presently seems to have had the closest encounter of the feline kind, on the night that she came home to her house by Ollersett Moor and found it occupied by a smooth-skinned, jet-black cat the size of an Alsatian dog. It had yellow eyes and a foul stench.

This was 26 March 1992 and, for some time, the animal was spitting and hissing inside Mrs Topliff's dining room. It then fled into the bedroom where she chased it with a broom handle! Before the cat scuttled downstairs and left via the window, Mrs Topliff was bitten and needed stitches in the wound.

This was apparently not the first time the animal had visited the Topliff household. She had chased it out before and, given that her house is surrounded by other buildings, this has led some experts to doubt the theory that the animal is a big cat, since these prefer not to go where people are.

The common theory for many big cat sightings is that they are simply mistaken identity for large domestic cats gone wild, or a rogue labrador, which can seem cat-like. Few witnesses are persuaded of that.

One of the few photographs of Britain's biggest big cat. Is this the sort of animal stalking the moors around New Mills?

Some researchers feel that the animals are more supernatural than zoological, because of their remarkable ability to vanish like a ghost. There have never been any carcasses or bones found which might suggest a real colony. However, the New Mills panther does have that fuzzy photograph and obvious physical evidence in bite marks and footprints to strongly suggest it is more than just an apparition.

The Derbyshire peaks near New Mills also host one of Britain's least known wildlife treasures. This is a colony of wallabies (which resemble small kangaroos). These seem to have thrived on the moors after some were released from a private collection. Experts believe as many as 30 may exist.

It is possible that big cats such as puma or panther owe their origins to similar escapees and that was certainly the case regarding Stockport's most astonishing mystery moggie in May 1983.

This turned up in Adswood, one of the most densely populated estates in the town and the last place anyone would expect to find a puma. But that is exactly what Margaret O'Malley did do. It was sitting on her garden shed, tamely accepting a saucer of milk while police were called. Eventually a woman rode up on horse-back and rounded up the animal which had run off from a nearby travelling circus.

At least this big cat was no spectral visitor nor a misperceived black dog or bedraggled pussy. Whether the creature that stalks New Mills will succumb to resolution quite so readily is another matter altogether.

A circular tour of Marple

Crop circles have been one of the most notorious of recent phenomena, big news around the world and hailed as mysterious messages about the fate of the Earth. Then, in September 1991, two artists revealed that they had faked many of these masterpieces and the game seemed to be up. Those peculiar patterns gouged into the world's crop fields were all the result of human engineering – a polite word that circle researchers use for hoaxing.

However, it is not quite that simple. There are reports of circles dating from the year 1590, and an ancient English woodcut from 1678 that seems to describe them as the work of a 'mowing devil'. This was long before the tabloid press or television discovered them and implies that the modern hoax may have merely duplicated an existing phenomenon. Indeed, the confessed hoaxers admit they got the idea from real circles they chanced to see which formed in Queensland, Australia in 1966.

Behind all the ballyhoo Marple Bridge hides one of the most important cases of crop circle activity. It arrived unheralded in a field containing a Strines farmer's loose hay, sloping down towards the River Goyt.

It occurred on 15 June 1988 as two seemingly unrelated incidents which were, in fact, tied closely together without most witnesses realising.

At 11am the deputy head of All Saints Primary School and some nearby school children, observed hay rising into the air. Thinking they were causing the havoc by tossing it about he went to tell them off, only to realise that the hay had been sucked up from a field beyond the school fence and the children had simply been staring in amazement. The force responsible is called a 'fairweather whirlwind', which on hot days can cause hay, grass, straw or even rubbish to spiral into the air.

All Saints' School, Marple Ridge. The strange whirlwind sucked up hay by the fence and carried it aloft over the trees in the background to rain down on the golf course beyond. (Jenny Randles)

At 12.45 that same day more pupils and a teacher playing rounders in the school grounds saw hay rising upwards again. Yet this time it did not disperse and fall quickly back to earth. It rotated into a tight corkscrew and solidified as a lens shape some 20 feet in diameter. This was dark black silhouetted against the bright sky and resembled for all the world a flying saucer.

Having risen vertically to above rooftop height the discus stopped climbing and began to drift slowly with the wind on a horizontal path across the school grounds. As it passed directly above the witnesses they felt a downward pressure on their heads and shoulders, suggesting that the hay was being kept aloft by a balance of upward and downward forces, including gravity, of course. 'Funny – like a soft wind', is how one described the sensation.

The astonished watchers in the school last saw the lens shape disappear over the steeple of the adjacent church with bits falling off the edges as if rapidly losing energy. However, an examination of the ground in the field beneath where the hay had been sucked up revealed that it was swirled into a small spiral circle of loose straw and grass, which unfortunately was blown out by the wind before anybody could photograph it.

The second phase involved residents of the housing estate on the far side of the school, astride a steep hill containing a golf course sloping towards Hazel Grove.

Here many people, unaware of what had occurred in the school grounds, saw a large mass resembling a swirling flock of birds separating out into a series of smaller ovals which rotated around one another 'like galaxies in the universe', as one woman termed it. These rained debris on the ground in a weird dark shower burst. People who examined this found it to be small clumps of hay with the stems twisted looking not unlike birds nests.

As the rapidly reducing clouds of hay moved down the slope, sprinkling their content onto the golf course, the size gradually reduced to nothing. The movement was slow and silent, little more than walking pace, with the hay clouds being kept aloft by weakening atmospheric forces. Eventually these dispersed leaving no trace that anything strange had happened.

This experience tells us something very important; that the real crop circle cases are the products of wind-borne forces. It also may provide a crucial clue to the nature of some UFO sightings, which would quite literally be a solution that is up in the air.

Marple marvels

Crop circles appear in areas frequented by other strange phenomena. Researchers call these 'window areas'. Marple is certainly the 'window' in the Stockport district and the place to be if you want to see odd things.

At the far end of the golf course that was sprinkled from the sky by descending hay is a frequented fishing pool. Here on 6 June 1976 two youths spotted a pair of white lights side by side above Wood Farm. Thinking these were just aircraft lights they were relieved to hear the sound of engines but turning around, saw that the aircraft was actually behind, following its normal path towards the airport. The lights that were ahead of them, moving slowly in their direction, made absolutely no sound at all.

As these passed overhead, their colour suddenly deepened to a blood red. Then, the objects arced around an electricity pylon as if tied to it by a rope and sailed off towards Hazel Grove where they promptly disappeared.

Directly across the valley and the Goyt from where the circle formed is Bottom's Hall. Here on 5 July 1977 another strange event took place.

A group of children beside the lake at 11pm reported to the adults in charge a peculiar light in the south east. They all watched it dance above the lake for some time, spreading out into an oval shape and turning dark orange. Then it simply disappeared.

However, the most intriguing case was on 4 March 1968 when a man was driving his Triumph Spitfire near Brown Low just north of Mellor when he spotted a golden ball of light speeding along the valley from the New Mills area and heading smoothly north towards Werneth Low. As it drifted past his car the radio suddenly cut out and the headlights and engine failed. Moments later the vehicle shuddered to a halt.

Seconds after this, with the golden light disappearing to the north, the car's electrical systems sprang back to life. The driver could now restart the engine and continue his journey. But the radio still did not work. His brother-in-law chanced to be a TV repairman and tried to fix the almost brand new set, but failed. However, the car was trouble free over the next two years until sold.

In 1978 the failed radio was analysed by ufologist, Roy Dutton and found to have blown two transistors, perhaps through a massive power surge. Once these were replaced the set worked perfectly.

The Hyde poltergeist

If we trace the course of the Mersey's other tributary, the Tame, south from Tameside into Stockport we find that it has also been host to many more strange happenings.

Mr and Mrs Farris* bought a corner shop in Hyde. What followed is an example of the mixture of both the frightening and the absurd which constitutes a typical poltergeist outbreak.

Between 1989 and 1991 they were working to renovate the old millstone grit gable end and the strangest of the events seemed to coincide with their attempts to alter the structure. When Mr Farris began to tinker with the brickwork, that act seemed to unleash forces trapped in the building that had stood undisturbed for more than a century.

Objects would move about on their own. However, often this would be in an amusing manner. For example, Mrs Farris was amazed to find cans of soft drink removed from the shop and lined up neatly across the floor. Once, she went out for just 20 minutes and returned to find all her saucepans extracted from the shelving and set up along the kitchen in perfect order, with the handles all pointing the same way and in precise sequence from the smallest to the largest. These were all presided over by her wok which stood 'like a sergeant major instructing soldiers on parade'.

While such events upset the family pets, they merely puzzled the occupants. However, the dogs were in turn unaffected by the terrifying apparitions that filled the store.

An old man in Victorian clothing was seen sitting in an armchair and smirking at them. On another occasion a figure in a long overcoat sailed across the bedroom in the middle of the night. A child was also seen.

The most disturbing incident of all occurred when the building next door caught fire and the frantic rescuers saw two children peering out of the upstairs window of the corner shop. Convinced they were really trapped the men tried to break in and free the victims, but there was nobody on that floor of the building. Indeed Mr and Mrs Farris had no children in the house at all and the only occupants were themselves, asleep on the floor above.

Happily, the commotion of this aborted rescue attempt was enough to awaken Mr and Mrs Farris from their deep slumber. As a result they evacuated the haunted corner shop and escaped the possible ravages of fire.

Wonders of Werneth Low

Across the Tame from Hyde is Haughton Green, formerly part of Manchester. Here on 24 December 1974 a strange sight was witnessed by a housewife who was admiring the frost over Werneth Low.

This country park and hall sit astride a hill and are seen from miles around. Over the years it has been at the centre of many unusual light phenomena and electrical effects on house lighting and passing cars. Yet oddly only one woman reported the vision which took place there that Christmas Eve.

It was a fresh winter's morning at 7.30am when she saw an oval mass rise from the hill and stretch out into an elongated cigar. Then, as if it were a child blowing soap bubbles, tiny opaque objects emerged from the end and floated across the sky. These headed southwards in the direction of Marple Bridge.

This phenomenon is known as a 'cloud cigar' and is best remembered for a case at Oloron in France in October 1952 when a meteorologist saw such a wonder of nature and was utterly perplexed by it. The cause remains a mystery. At Oloron tiny slivers of white-flecked material drifted down towards the ground in imitation of a snow fall which received the name "angel hair". This same thing has been duplicated on a number of occasions since in France and Japan; although usually when analysed, the material deposited over trees and telephone wires, turns out to be spiders web. Not that this explains what the substance is doing falling down from a cigar in the sky.

There was no angel hair on Werneth Low that Christmas Eve but in all other respects the cloud cigar was the same phenomenon as at Oloron. Indeed, it vanished by merging into the rocks on the top of the hillside, suggesting to some that this is where its origin lay, as a form of plasma generated from within the Pennine landscape.

Strange drifting green lights have been seen atop Werneth Low on other occasions and have been chased by police patrols and spotted by aircraft on their way in to Manchester Airport. A particular example caused quite a furore around the golf course when the little ball whizzed across one of the greens.

There could certainly be worse places to sit out and watch the stars. Searching for strangers in the night.

Stockport's haunted castle

Few people realise that Stockport once had a castle, but that is how Castle Street in Edgeley earned its name. Today it is little more than a busy shopping centre in the shadows of Stockport County football stadium.

The name Edgeley itself is interesting. This is the first district through which the fledgling and now united River Mersey passes; although others might argue that this honour really goes to the Hollywood area (another of the town's little known attributes!).

The term 'ley' has several derivations in the English language. One of these is from lea (or field) but another is believed to come from an ancient British term meaning linear alignment.

Recently, earth mystery students looking at what are called 'leys' (often misinterpreted as 'ley lines', which is redundant terminology since a ley is a line) have rediscovered what they think the ancient peoples knew thousands of years ago. You can plot onto a map a series of straight lines that pass through important points, often demarcated by burial mounds, stone circles, and in later centuries churches or castles.

Opinion is divided about what these alignments mean. Some say that they were nothing but artificial pathways marked onto the landscape, possibly for spiritual or meditational purposes. Others suggest that some hidden power or latent energy within the earth itself was tapped by leys which serve as veins to channel it through the living biosphere of the planet. Certainly, there are similar systems in other parts of the world. In China they are called dragon lines, for example.

Either way Edgeley appears to rest upon a ley which also passes through Marple ridge and other regions of extreme activity in the Mersey Valley. It moves westward out towards Risley Moss, where many strange things have also occurred.

A pub now sits near where the castle was in Edgeley. Here in May 1988 a birthday party was rudely interrupted by a ghost! In fact, a man who was taking photographs of the celebrations found that two of his pictures had a weird looking white filament of light on them, like a spectral hand draped across the shot. Nobody saw anything odd at the time. Although some argue that this was merely a processing fault on the film, there have been quite a few strange lights in the sky from this ley focal point too – so who knows?

Ello, Ello, a UFO

Possibly the best known UFO cases near Stockport occurred a short hop down the river at Cheadle Heath. Unfortunately, the case does not live up to its much vaunted reputation; although it does have an interesting tale behind it.

It occurred on 31 January 1988 at 6.22am when two police officers on patrol from Cheadle Hulme were sitting in a car near the start of Bird Hall Lane. The night was dark and quiet, when they saw a strange light ahead of them which seemed stationary in the sky. They were puzzled, especially when it resolved into a triangle of three lights and began to move on a descending path to the south west, dipping below houses and out of sight in the general direction of the Mersey.

Later in the day, the two officers did make enquiries at Manchester Airport to see if they had recorded anything unusual on their radar screens. They had not done so and, superficially, that seems to imply that the case must be quite significant. What goes unsaid here is that the radar had recorded *something,* but it was simply not something that was unusual; hence the reply. Infact it had recorded an aircraft, one of many that cross this area on the final glide path into Manchester.

Of course, police officers in this part of Stockport are more than used to seeing aircraft pass overhead, so there had to be more to it than that. Indeed there was. This was a British Airways Tristar jet landing after a flight from New York. Although these do come to Manchester they are not the sort of aircraft many would be familiar with, especially in the dark, and they do have an unusual lighting system which can easily look like a triangle if seen from a certain angle.

In other words, the police officers described what they saw quite well and are not to be blamed for the excesses of the media who later got hold of the story and made more out of it than was ever there.

Next day, the police considered holding a press conference on the case. But it was realised that news sources were likely to treat the sighting in a less than sober fashion and that the probable explanation was not what most of them wanted to hear.

The case featured in several newspapers and eventually flashed around the world, not always with the facts well presented. This was largely because the police officers had wisely chosen not to get involved, but that did not stop the media bandwagon rolling.

We spent some time dealing with one TV crew who intended to use the story, come what may. The police officers being incommunicado meant that they needed to find other angles. We refused to be drawn into this and turned down an offer to appear on screen discussing how a policeman in West Yorkshire had once told of being abducted by little entities. It hardly seemed relevant and we simply wanted to relate the facts about this case. They served as a timely warning that people often see something strange in the sky, but that does not necessarily mean that the Martians have landed!

Since the TV crew did not even know where the sighting had taken place and we were not about to enlighten them under the circumstances, they chose to take some film of the town centre miles from where the incident had occurred. The reporter told us that nobody watching would know the difference!

So it was that Stockport's great close encounter came to achieve fame and notoriety, despite never being a candidate for the UFO event of the year. However, while this incident may not have been as spectacular as the headlines might have led many to think, there was a case that no media source ever published which was very puzzling indeed . . .

I am a camera

Only a few hundred yards from the scene where the two police officers had their sighting in 1988 there was a quite remarkable and utterly unheralded close encounter.

Keith Rogers* had worked with the electricity board and been a service engineer with the RAF. So he knew what was flying around and what had no business being up in the sky.

One evening in April 1975 he was walking to the local pub (he stresses that he was going there and not coming back!). He was in a part of Adswood where a bridge crosses an old railway line heading south, opposite the excavations of the brick works. Suddenly he saw a streak of green light approach along the track from the north, heading extremely fast in his direction.

Stunned by this Keith stood in amazement as the light zipped to an instant halt so close that he could almost reach out and touch it. Silhouetted by the glow of a street lamp just behind him, it was now seen to be a very unusual object.

It was like a cruise missile, sleek and black. In the centre, like an evil eye, was an oval green patch. A cover, or lid, was rising from this to reveal the green light more clearly. The impression created was of a huge flying camera that was endeavouring to take photographs of him, though that seems absurd given the circumstances.

During this experience Keith experienced what we call the Oz Factor, the total disappearance of all people and passing traffic. The entire suburban area was plunged into an eerie silence which made the whole experience even more frightening.

He stared at the object, only a couple of feet in length, for what must have been about 10 seconds. He does regret not walking under it and looking at the far side, something he feels that he could have very easily done. Keith was too entranced by the sight of the extraordinary phenomenon which was so improbable in this urbanised area.

Then the shutter closed over the eye again, which was swallowed behind the blackness of the cigar shape, leaving only a dim glow. As if its mission were completed the object then sped away like a bullet to the south, towards Macclesfield and over the brick works. In a matter of seconds it had completely disappeared.

"What was powering and controlling this thing?" the witness asked us, unable to resolve such questions for himself. He was aware that the military sometimes operate what are called RPVs (remotely piloted vehicles) – like very sophisticated model aircraft. These are used for reconnaissance purposes in areas where it might be dangerous to send in a surveillance helicopter because of enemy action.

However, it seems unlikely that an RPV as advanced as this one could have been in operation in 1975. Anyhow, what possible interest could there be in a back street in Stockport? There does not appear to be much terrorist activity on the streets of Adswood.

Of course, possibly it had come from somewhere very different. One suggestion was that people from elsewhere had sent a remote-control, time-travel probe to look at life on Earth in the late twentieth century. If so, then perhaps the tourist board in Stockport might like to ponder the thought that someone, from somewhere, seemed to have been very interested in paying their town a visit!

2

SOUTH MANCHESTER MEANDERS

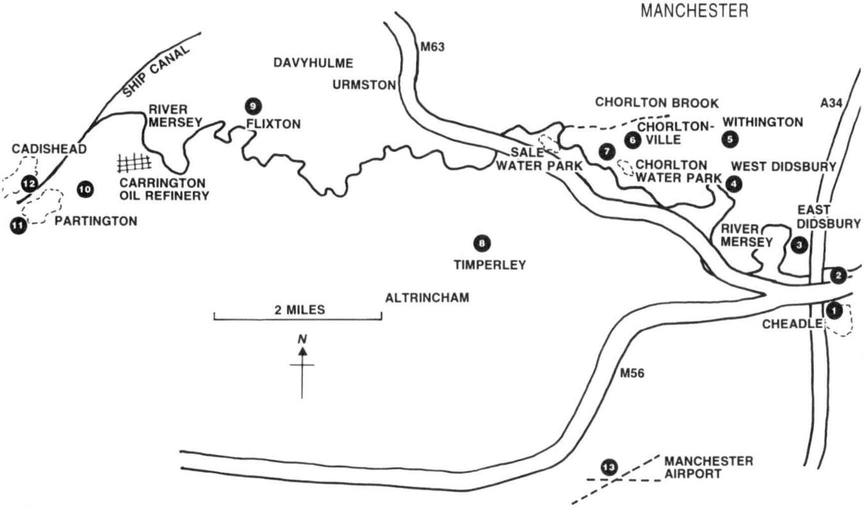

1.	Cheadle Cross Ghost	2.	Abney Hall Phantom Ninjas
3.	East Didsbury UFO Abduction	4.	West Didsbury Ice Fall
5.	The Hum	6.	Hough End Hall Ghost Music
7.	Chorlton Marshes Ghosts	8.	Timperley Poltergeist
9.	Davyhulme Sunset Mystery	10.	Carrington UFO
11.	Green Fireballs	12.	Cadishead Alien Contact
13.	Manchester Airport Ghosts (see chapter 3)		

The Floodplains of South Manchester and North Cheshire

After leaving Stockport, the Mersey meanders on a journey that takes it from Cheadle to Carrington across lush green land. It moves westward through districts of southern Manchester on the northern bank and the stockbroker countryside of north Cheshire, to be found on the south. The river continued to form the traditional divide between the two counties for centuries and traces of this still linger.

The land surrounding the river has been quite cleverly utilised in recent times, for golf courses and more appropriately the water parks at Sale and Chorlton. These have become popular for day trippers and family outings alike. But they have their stranger side as well!

The M63 motorway follows the Mersey Valley for some way out of Stockport, through Cheadle and into Sale. It allows rapid access to many sites featured in this section of the book. Eventually it splits in two, with the M56 motorway heading to the south and west towards the distant Wirral and north Wales, and the M63 itself staking a claim northwards for the latter day marvel of the bridge over the Ship Canal near Irlam. This can be seen from some distance, spread out as if created by a child's construction kit. It strides over the canal with arrogance.

After fording the bridge, the M62 is soon met. Already well through its coast-to-coast trek from Hull, this takes the traveller westward towards the setting sun of maritime endeavour that is the port of Liverpool.

We try to locate many of the stories that we relate within reach of both the M56 and the M62. You will notice that there are some fascinating things that take place in this busily urbanised area. So follow the course of the Mersey as it skirts well south of Manchester city centre, almost as if avoiding the noise and fumes up there, and see just what is really going on within modern suburbia.

The ghosts of Cheadle cross

Cheadle cross can be found just off the M63 near where the old railway line still passes. A curious incident took place right here.

Sandra Thompson* was returning from a dance in south Manchester one day in the mid 1970s. It was very late, around 2am. The roads were of course quite deserted. Her husband was driving the car, concentrating on little else but getting home and then to bed.

Suddenly a figure appeared ahead of them in the road. It was a woman who had just stepped out right into their path, luckily avoiding them. She looked old and quite frail and Mrs Thompson not surprisingly got out to make absolutely sure that she was all right after the ordeal.

Her husband was a bit perplexed by this, asking what his wife was fussing about, but Mrs Thompson felt it right not to let this woman wander around on her own at such a late hour.

The woman, who appeared at least 90 years old, said only that she was very grateful for this kindness and indicated where she wished to go. Mrs Thompson went with her to the Lime Grove cottages at the back of the Tesco supermarket, leading her by the arm across the road. Throughout this procedure there was absolutely nothing strange about the incident at all.

At the cottage gates the old woman went towards the house. Mrs Thompson briefly looked away and lent forward slightly to let her pass. Her eyes were averted for no more than a few seconds, but when she glanced back the old lady was nowhere in sight.

With her heart thumping, Sandra Thompson returned her view to the house to which she had just led the vanishing woman. It was boarded up and shuttered over, as if it had not been lived in for quite some time. The woman whom she had helped towards it could not possibly have lived there.

Enquiries have suggested that an old woman had lived in these houses for many years earlier in this century. Did her spirit somehow still cling to the area? If so, this is one of the rare occasions where a phantom interacts with living people, avoiding the popular sceptical opinion that it is just a hallucination. The woman that Sandra Thompson helped across the road was as large as life – suffering from only one problem, apparently she was not really alive after all!

Ninja dwarves on the rampage

If you leave Cheadle cross and head towards the B5095 over both the M63 and the Mersey you pass Abney Hall. You might miss it, opposite an exclusive hospital, because it lies secluded behind some bushes, a bit like an unexpected oasis in a desert.

In the daytime there are pleasant walks and gardens, making for a relaxing few hours; but the Gothic imagery of the mansion looks very imposing, not to say frightening, in the dark. So it is easy to understand why it should have generated a spooky tale. It is a bizarre story, involving phantoms the like of which we have never come across before.

It began in the summer of 1988 when a group of teenagers was taking martial arts classes with adult instructors. The idea was to bottle up the emotions and energy and release this in a controlled way by use of large poles and swift movements. However, things started to go badly wrong and their outdoor Sunday night sessions were rudely interrupted by a terrible presence.

At first, a foot was seen in the bushes. When one of the men went to see who was playing a joke, no one was there. Experiences like that became more common as the nights began to draw in and the shadows danced on the shrubbery creating all-too-frightening images.

Much of the activity went on around a little waterfall in the grounds. Here, a figure was seen by the group which was small, squat and ugly in appearance. It wore clothing that resembled the dark suits that they donned for their activities; a sort of phantom ninja dwarf!

The entity was at first assumed to be human, but it was soon clear that this was no rival martial arts group playing a trick. The dwarf was seen to float up in the air from a rock upon which it sat. An intrepid group member went right up to it and saw nothing, but felt a pressure pushing at him, before he, not surprisingly, ran. Then it would vanish instantly and reappear in bushes some distance away, almost as if teasing the students.

Oddly, this did not scare them away. One of the girls told Roy Sandbach and ourselves that she felt the entity needed them to exist, as if drawing power from their spirit. The fact that it manifested in such an appropriate form suggests that there was some link of this sort. Ghostly ninja warriors are not a very common sight in Cheadle, or anywhere else for that matter!

However, the situation rapidly deteriorated. One girl was driven into a frenzy and attacked her boyfriend, others having to tear her away. Later she could not explain why she did it. Another saw a shape appear in front of her as she sat on a bench. It came as if set to throttle the life out of her.

Worst of all was what happened to one of the teachers. He found himself confronting an unseen force which crushed down on him and he ran, then crawled away towards the little pond in the grounds as if to hurl himself in. He had to be dragged away by some of the students, who by now were in no mood to continue these nocturnal nightmares and found another venue.

Abney Hall was a riverside mansion built by a Manchester cotton baron but in more recent times it has been used for council offices. It also has a reputation for being haunted by a woman, seen over many years. There have been other tales of room lights switching themselves on and off and of guard dogs being suddenly terrified. Legend has it, rather improbably, that the spectre might be the mistress of mystery, Agatha

The waterfall in the grounds of Abney Hall where the phantom Ninja warrior dwarf appeared in 1988. He would sit on the rocks and terrify onlookers. (Jenny Randles)

Christie. She had stayed at the hall and, rumour says, may even have been there during her infamous and still unsolved temporary disappearance, reconstructed in the movie *Agatha*.

At the time of the ninja warrior encounters building work was going on in the hall grounds. The area is set on sandy rock, the quartz rich sandstone through which the Mersey cuts its path across Stockport. It even has caves that were used as shelters during the war. As noted, quartz rock has an affinity with strange phenomena, possibly because it might generate an electric spark when put under pressure by building work or bodies of water, for instance. At Abney Hall the builders certainly had a shock one day.

In November 1988, soon after the teacher's awful encounter, the ground suddenly vibrated for some seconds as if hit by a major earthquake. The contractors even checked with the seismology unit at Edinburgh to see if it was safe to continue work. It was. There had been no tremor. However, the shaking seemed to wring the last drops of energy from the ground and the Ninja warrior sightings ended with this appropriate send off.

Taken for a ride

A little further west from Cheadle the Mersey's course curves through East Didsbury, the final outpost of Manchester's housing. Here, on the sunny evening of 19 August 1979, Linda Jones and her two children, a teenage girl and her five year old son, were spending an hour picking wild flowers on the river banks beside the open land enclosed by the looping river. But they were not prepared for the event about to shatter this idyllic summer scene.

The first thing that they became aware of was a flash of light to the north and west over Didsbury golf course. At first they assumed it was one of the many aircraft that pass over the area, but then they realised it was something quite different. There was a mixture of pink and orange behind the silver, possibly caused by reflections from the setting sun, and a curious object was descending towards the open ground to their east. If it was an aircraft then it seemed about to crash.

Filled with excitement and panic they scrambled up the gorse-strewn embankment, an act which took a couple of minutes. Once on top of the rise they had an excellent view towards where the object had seemingly descended. It now appeared to be hovering just above ground level.

In appearance it resembled a gondola or boat, with a curved base and a girder-like structure. But there was a reddish glow on top. Both curious and puzzled, they set off towards it, the children noting a strange fixation in their mother's eyes as if she was being drawn to the thing.

The next they knew they were running away, the grass around them swaying as if in a fierce wind. The object was now flying silently behind an inbound aircraft, passing over undisturbed houses. Linda stumbled as she ran and hurt her ankle, having to be helped home by the children. The indigo sky was turning darker, but this fact did not immediately register as odd.

On entering the house, they were greeted by Mr Jones who put a question that in retrospect seems bizarre. Looking at his wife's ankle he asked, "who did that to you – a spaceman?" He later said it was a joke that just popped into his mind. However, even stranger was that he was in the house at all. Mrs Jones says they had first seen the object, only minutes before, at what she estimates was about 9pm and yet her husband was on shift work that night until 10pm!

Of course, none of the family was watching the time while picking flowers nor when observing the strange object. Mr Jones also told Jenny Randles that he might possibly have got home as early as 9.30pm that night, but either way there did seem to be a period of time unaccounted for.

Over the days following the encounter, Linda and her daughter both developed strange weals on their legs, which faded after a few days. Mrs Jones also had a redness beneath the eyes. Their young son had strange nightmares about men with heads shaped like raindrops. He was calling the object a 'crashed boat' and from the moment he got home had been urging his father to take him back into the fields to see it.

Determined to do something about the matter, they eventually came into contact with a local UFO investigator; he arranged regression hypnosis with a doctor in St John's Street, which is Manchester's equivalent of London's Harley Street. This was carried out only on Linda and her daughter, their son was thought to be too young for the experiment.

This kind of work has been conducted on hundreds of witnesses all over the world who suffer strange time lapses during encounters of this sort. Repeatedly, these reveal near-identical stories about spacenapping. The problem is that hypnosis can stimulate recall just as it can trigger vivid fantasies. This is well illustrated by the stage hypnotists who coerce their victims into seeing all manner of things. It is usually impossible, even for the witnesses, to make the distinction, since all they can do is relate the images that appear in their minds.

Limited information was revealed under hypnosis by Linda and her daughter; although Linda did see several strange beings with 'puppet like' faces and described how she was probed on a long table or bed by some sort of light. The word 'Algenyon' appeared in her mind, but she does not know why.

Certainly this example of an alien abduction is quite typical of those from around the world where people feel that they were taken for a ride and then brought back again (as dramatised by the hit 1993 movie *Fire in the Sky*). The quiet and otherwise tranquil Didsbury suburbs hosted one of Britain's first cases to be explored in this way and, in that sense, may go down in history – although on which planet the history books will be published may be quite another matter!

One lump or two?

Some really strange things fall out of the sky. At Edgeley, Stockport, in 1992 a nut from an aircraft crashed into a garden and at Reddish, outside a local church, pennies literally from heaven made a curious descent.

These things are called fafrotskies (ie falls from the skies) by researchers into strange phenomena. The most common of these is the ice-bomb. This is like a very large hail stone, usually smashing down from a clear sky and heavy enough to do serious damage. Several houses have had holes smashed through their roofs and people have had narrow escapes.

Ideas about what ice bombs are vary; although there can be no doubting their reality as they leave behind very tangible effects. The most common theory is that they come from faulty aircraft toilets that deposit their content into the air to ultimately plop to earth. This freezes as it drops and leaves a big hole where it impacts. It has even been suggested for these holes that we adopt the term 'crop circle'; but change the 'o' into an 'a'.

Unfortunately, it is impossible to make this rational idea work, particularly as ice-bombs have rained down on us since long before we had aircraft, let alone aircraft lavatory systems. So another theory, from Dr Louis Frank, is that the bombs are ice comets from space that hit the upper atmosphere many times a day but rarely run the gauntlet to reach Earth.

Luckily, science was given a big boost by what may well be the most important ice-bomb that has so far fallen. It did so only a few hundred yards north of the Mersey, on Burton Road in West Didsbury. The impact occurred on the evening of 2 April 1973 a few minutes after a single flash of lightning (but no storm) had rent the skies of south Manchester. The huge mass of ice, weighing several pounds, struck the ground only 10 feet from a man walking home and then broke into large lumps. As chance had it, the near victim was Dr Richard Griffiths, a research scientist at the university!

With his good fortune staring at him from Burton Road, Dr Griffiths decided not to pick up all the melting evidence and collected just the largest lump. Storing this in his freezer he could then take it to the lab to do some tests. These revealed that it had formed in 51 separate layers, one on top of the other, trapping air bubbles as it fell. It had dropped a long way through the sky and was definitely not from an aircraft. How it had formed or what forces had kept it aloft for so long are unknown.

The Withington hum

Strange things go on in bedrooms late at night. This seems especially true within the Withington triangle, which also includes Didsbury and Rusholme. But perhaps the oddest nocturnal experience reported by the citizens here is the hum.

In October 1966 Marion Smith heard the hum from her home north of the Mersey beside Fog Lane Park. It started at around 2am and became so bad that she could not sleep for it. She described it as a penetrating, probing noise akin to an electricity sub station on overdrive crossed with a swarm of rampant bees nesting under the floorboards. The sound went on for long periods, then just disappeared.

Marion thought she was going mad and told her doctor that something was wrong with her ears. Neither was correct. Then the hum just went away.

However, Mrs Smith is not the only person in this area to have heard the hum. Indeed the records go back a long way. There are some suggestions that the hum was buzzing during the early eighteenth century and there was a discussion of it in the Manchester press in 1878. The name 'hummadruzz' was then coined, which was meant to describe how it resembles a combination of a humming, droning and buzzing. Nobody figured out what it was; although there were some interesting ideas about underground races living in caves who were tunnelling their way to the surface at night as part of some invasion plan! This seems most likely to have been conjured up by someone overdosing on H.G. Wells, the contemporary equivalent of too much *Star Trek* on TV.

In 1960 another outbreak of the hum hit Britain and the government mounted an investigation, sealing victims in soundproofed rooms to try to stop the onslaught. Some still heard it. New ideas were brought forward about pressurised water pipes, even electricity supply malfunctions, all irrelevant but suggested because few realised the hum was not a local or recent event.

The hum has occurred all over the world and keeps on happening. In 1992 there were waves of it in Alabama, USA, where mine shaft fans were falsely blamed, and near Stroud in Gloucestershire, where secret experiments at the Government's telecommunications HQ were wrongly suggested.

So, on your trek along the Mersey Valley, do stop off at Didsbury or Withington, listen carefully to the still night air – and wonder.

The spectral music of Hough End

As the Mersey flows west from Didsbury towards Sale it passes through Chorlton-cum-Hardy near Southern Cemetery, usually called 'the dead centre of Manchester'. Tucked away around the back of here where Chorlton brook flows into the Mersey off the ominously named Nell Lane, is a large imposing house with quite a reputation.

Hough End Hall is another of those typical old style family mansions dating from the time when the area surrounding the river was largely countrified and desirable as a retreat for the newly-rich of the industrial revolution. But the local youth recall it with another kind of affection.

During the 1950s it was said to house a phantom. Chris Robinson told us of the time when, as a youngster in about 1959, he was dared to face the spectre and soon regretted it.

That Hough End Hall was haunted was a popular rumour which probably relied more upon the antics of the teenagers of the day. As such, Chris was determined to break the mould and prove that the tales were nonsense.

He went late at night with a friend, who very soon deserted him, and stood there in front of the darkened building. There was much less traffic then than there is today and the street lighting was also inferior. But it was not the view of the building that was terrifying. It was the sounds that emerged from the direction of the hall, strange high pitched wails. They sounded rather like an organist in a frenzy, striking out with high notes carried by the wind in a fluttering crescendo. They chilled the blood. Chris stood his ground for a time but ultimately gave up and ran.

Others supposedly heard Hough End's phantom organist, although there do not seem to be any modern stories. The locals tended to be dismissive, suggesting that the marsh land around the Mersey played funny tricks on sounds and this may well have just been an acoustic echo or distortion of some more mundane noise, such as a choir at a church a mile away. But those who heard the spectral organist were not so easily persuaded. To them he was very real, or certainly surreal.

Whether the ghost was ever present or has since found peace, pay homage to this building if you can and imagine what it must have been like to stand there, dared to face a phantom that you did not believe in, and then . . .

Ghosts on Chorlton Marshes

If you move from Hough End Hall down Mauldeth Road through the pleasant village of Chorltonville and then head for the Mersey you strike some marsh land that is full of intrigue. This is a popular spot for walkers and joggers on a Sunday, with Sale Water Park just across the river. In contrast, there is a big sewage works waiting to greet you as well!

For many years there have been stories about a ghost light seen drifting by the river here. It is speculated to be the spirit of one of the several people who drowned on these marshes, possibly a suicide.

However, witnesses rarely see anything other than a pale, flickering yellow light and its association with a human ghost is less than clear. Some researchers have noted that boggy ground can produce rich methane (and the sewage works probably does not help much in that regard!). A combination known as marsh gas can incandesce in certain circumstances and be carried along by the wind like giant, floating candles, until the supply of fuel is exhausted and it then simply goes out.

This phenomenon is known from many similar marsh lands and over the years was given various names, such as 'Jack o' Lantern' and 'Will o' the Wisp'. It achieved a reputation as an evil spirit because those who were lured by it across the darkened countryside sometimes did not realise that they were heading straight for a river. When the light suddenly disappeared, they were sometimes trapped in the dark to be swallowed up by the waters.

It is quite possible that some of the Chorlton marshes suicides were no such thing. Today, of course, if this floating mass of burning gas is spotted we have our own interpretations for it (UFOs being one). But these are no less mysterious. We seem to prefer the supernatural to the rational.

Across the path that leads from Chorlton to Sale over the M63 is a little bridge (Jackson's Bridge) with a famous inn there, highly thought of by locals and visitors alike. Jackson's Boat Inn is, naturally enough, also haunted, but in a curious way. Several staff have reported seeing a man in full Scottish highland dress and the name 'George' was adopted by them to show that he was considered friendly, though a few bottles and glasses have been pushed around by an unseen force from time to time. The reason why such a strange phantom 200 miles south of Scotland is thought to haunt the building, is that the pub was a meeting place during the Jacobite rebellion.

Jackson's Boat Inn on the banks of the River Mersey; the inn is allegedly haunted by the apparition of a man in Scottish Highland dress and was, apparently, a meeting place during the Jacobite rebellion.(Peter Hough)

The house-proud poltergeist

Just south of Sale Water Park is Timperley, a suburb of the north Cheshire market town of Altrincham. Here, in 1984 something very strange took place in an ordinary semi-detached house. For a time it became anything but ordinary.

Ray Jones* was used to odd goings on. He had put up with a poltergeist for quite a long time and it had some quite infuriating habits.

Ray would come into the bedroom and find that coat hangars had been extracted from the wardrobe and lined up across the bed in geometrical precision. On another occasion he took his slippers off and averted his eyes for just a moment, looking back to find that these and other footwear had been neatly piled up on the carpet so that they all touched one another in a long line.

Whoever or whatever was doing this was obsessed with neatness and seemingly did not have much regard for Ray's penchant for sneaking the occasional glance at a girlie magazine. At least that is how Ray came to interpret the actions of his house-proud, if invisible, cohabitant.

Ray loved to play Scrabble with his home computer. In this game, letters are dealt, like playing cards, and each player must use them to maximum effect, creating words to fit in a crossword-like grid making use of the letters placed by other participants. The one with the highest score eventually wins.

In computer Scrabble the machine is the opponent and uses its memory to access words from a dictionary and put down the ones that score the most in any given situation. But Ray found that, rather than doing this, his computer was acting like an oracle, answering questions in his mind with highly appropriate words. Whenever he would have a quick peak at a magazine while waiting for the computer to find the next word (and they can take a notoriously long time) he would return to the screen to find that it had laid down something like 'naughty', as if issuing a mild reproof for his intervening actions! Ray soon learnt not to do it any more.

However, on the morning of 31 October 1984 things took a more dramatic turn when Ray was to have a visual encounter with something in his house that was not at all what he was expecting. It was no ghost, more akin to an extra-terrestrial version of entertainer Bruce Forsythe!

Ray awoke in the early morning, just after 6am as his bedside clock showed him. He just knew that something was wrong. Sure enough, as he looked up from the sheets he could see a weird figure bending over the table at the side of the bed and examining the clock radio.

Instantly Ray knew this was no ordinary person. It was quite small, maybe four feet tall or just over, and almost insect like in structure. The head was domed and the resemblance to Bruce Forsythe came specifically in the chin area, being the entertainer's famed trademark, which in this non-human intruder was equally prominent and angular.

The entity was wearing a black all-over suit that covered the face completely. As a graphic designer it was this clothing that particularly impressed Ray. He says that he would have loved to have taken out a patent in the material, which stretched like nylon, had the texture of rubber but was gently ribbed like corduroy.

The most difficult thing to understand was how the entity had ever gotten into the suit. Ray noticed that the neck was much too thin to support a head that was too large in relation to the rest of the body. It teetered like a pumpkin on a stick. The neck-hole would have had to stretch an incredible amount for the creature to have taken it off again.

As he took this in, Ray also noticed something important. As wide awake as he knew he was, and as real as this seemed to be, he thought that it might be a hallucination. Something like this could not really be there in his room. But then he realised that he was unconsciously screwing up his eyes to look at the figure. He let the muscles relax and the entity went out of focus. This was because he was near sighted and usually wore glasses. Yet, surely, he reasoned to himself, if this were some sort of hallucination, it would not be seen by the eyes but in his mind. In which case how could it be distorted by his poor eyesight?

Just as he worked this out the entity vanished. One microsecond it was there, the next it was gone. The white of the wall behind rushed in to fill his vision and Ray now thought of another problem. His eyes had told him that there really was someone in the room but, if so, this sudden disappearance would have left a vacuum in the room space. Air should have rushed in to fill the gap and he would have felt a breeze. He felt nothing.

All Ray could do was describe what happened and wonder who, or what, he had run into that hallowe'en morning.

A rather amazing sunset

The sunsets over Flixton are quite spectacular, or at least the one witnessed by the Wellingtons* on 21 July 1978 was.

They lived in Davyhulme, between the M63 and the Mersey where, having flowed through Sale, it is about to join forces with the Manchester Ship Canal and run as one waterway in the direction of Warrington.

Mrs Wellington saw the phenomenon first and was astonished at its beauty. It was over the river, to the south and west, at about 10.15pm on a hot day. Calling to her husband he searched the house for some binoculars, eventually finding them and rushing out to join her. The thing was still in the sky when he got there, although it was fading.

When first seen by Mrs Wellington it had covered a large expanse of the twilight sky with a huge dark central dome that was surrounded by an aura of around 30 to 40 purple rays. These emerged like spokes from a wheel shooting out about 12 times the diameter of the central hub.

After about 90 seconds the phenomenon began to collapse in upon itself, with one ray after another entering the hub like a porcupine drawing in its quills. Eventually they all disappeared and the central mass popped out of existence. During the entire experience, Mrs Wellington, a very artistic soul, had been entranced. Indeed she went through the Oz Factor, with all environmental sounds vanishing. Davyhulme had come to a complete standstill for two or three minutes. Normally busy streets were temporarily deserted.

The Wellingtons wanted to be reassured that they had seen something explicable. So they wrote to TV astronomer, Patrick Moore, who was kind enough to write back and suggest that they had witnessed a bright meteor. They happily accepted this solution, even though it seems to us to be virtually impossible. Meteors are not visually like this spectacle and do not hover for several minutes in one part of the sky.

More likely, this was a very rare atmospheric phenomenon such as has been seen in the tropics, albeit rarely. It seems to connect with dust particles in the upper atmosphere creating a kaleidoscopic distortion on the setting sun's rays. But why did it happen that night in Davyhulme and why did no other people report seeing such a marvellous sight?

A refined UFO

South of Flixton is the big expanse of Carrington Moss upon which sits a gigantic oil refinery. Next to this is the housing estate overspill of Partington.

The burn off from Carrington is visible on some nights as far north as the East Lancs Road and there have been spurious UFO sightings made when car drivers have deserted their vehicles to wander across fields looking at the flickering orange mass on the horizon to their south east.

However, Carrington has attracted several puzzling encounters. It is almost as if someone is very interested in the industrial technology that seethes within its confines.

A former RAF pilot, driving on the road from Carrington towards Lymm in 1977, spotted three green spheres of light shooting across the sky like comets.

Green fireballs like these are amazingly common around industrial complexes. Between 1948 and 1952 they were seen by many scientists in

Green fireballs like these are amazingly common around industrial complexes. Between 1948 and 1952 they were seen by many scientists in New Mexico. Many had top security clearances, because the lights flew over secret research establishments such as Los Alamos. The Pentagon feared spying missions from some unknown source. Physicists of the calibre of Oppenheimer and Teller, fathers of the atom bomb, were involved in Project Twinkle, created to find the answer. Monitor cameras were set up, but when these were established in an area where the green fireballs flew, they moved to another spot nearby and so avoided being captured on film. Some data was gathered, including a spectral analysis that showed how the fireballs glowed green because of copper in their make-up.

Green fireballs have appeared around other oil refineries, including Stanlow near Ellesmere Port. They also plagued the area around the Sizewell nuclear power station in Suffolk. Residents who live near Carrington are apparently quite used to their presence. When June Firswood* first moved to Partington her neighbour asked what she thought about the 'flying thingies' there. Puzzled, June asked for an elaboration, only to be told that strange lights were often seen over the refinery but nobody discussed them.

On 14 November 1977, some seven years after this conversation, June had cause to remember it and fortunately did talk about it, to ourselves and fellow investigator Ron Sargeant.

June was boosted by the fact that there were three others with her at the time when she saw this thing. They were people she knew by sight, but not by name, as they all got off a bus from Manchester about the same time each evening. As they walked from the stop towards Partington at about 5.45pm that night they saw a huge light drifting towards them from Carrington Moss and heading across the refinery in the direction of Irlam.

At first they assumed it was a new floodlight within the oil complex, but they soon realised that it was in the sky. It drifted in eerie silence at a sedate pace, passing directly overhead.

By now it was visible as a huge rectangular mass with two white lights set behind grills at the front and a throbbing red light at the rear. It moved so slowly that it seemed to take ages to pass overhead, time slowing to a crawl and the Oz Factor striking again. Everyone was astonished, more so later when it was realised that half of Greater

Manchester had not seen this thing, as expected. All those who watched it head off to cross the Mersey were adamant that it was several football fields in length.

The matter was reported to the police by June, and Sergeant Butts arrived on the scene at 7pm. He attested to us that she was genuinely shocked. He had little doubt that she had seen something that had really scared her. But where had it gone to after passing the oil refinery? It was rush-hour and it should have flown over Irlam, a town with tens of thousands of people. How could there be no other witnesses?

Butts told us six months later, when we first heard about the case, that he remembered it well, because he had been unable to resolve it. Hoping it might be an aircraft or airship he had contacted the airport less than two hours after the sighting had occurred. They knew nothing, pointing out that their radar clearly recorded the oil refinery but had tracked nothing passing over it that evening. Butts interest in the case was fired when he discovered that two police officers at Sale had seen the thing from Washway Road. He looked up their sketches and compared them with those from the bus passengers at Carrington. They clearly depicted the same object.

Sergeant Butts said that enquiries revealed there were so many lights in the area that suspicions had even been entertained about illegal helicopter flights. But this was not proven. In truth the mystery remained. He passed the case to the Ministry of Defence who, if they made any discoveries about it, told neither witnesses nor the police.

The ministers from Mars

One of June Firswood's 'flying thingies' seems to have made its way across the Mersey and landed on the far bank near the chemical works at Cadishead. At least, that is one way of interpreting the extraordinary story of Edward Dutton*

In January 1983, Ed had just bought an old motorcycle from a friend in Salford. However, as it was untaxed he decided to take it to the banks of the Mersey canal so that he could try it out off the road. He carefully wheeled it there at about 9pm and then set it up on its stand. Before he started to tinker with the machinery he decided he had need to relieve

Two figures were peering over his motorcycle. Assuming them to be youths bent on no good he shouted at them, but they ignored him completely. So Ed now shouted again, in more animated and colourful terms this time, as he made his way towards them. He almost immediately regretted his choice of (mostly four letter) words because on closer inspection the two men appeared to be church ministers!

This interpretation was forced upon him by the dark suits they wore, with what looked like a white collar round their neck. But if they were vicars, they were very odd ones. They looked like identical twins and were smiling at him in grotesque fashion as they stroked the seat of the motorbike in perfect unison!

The Oz factor now took hold. Sounds vanished, time became confused and the next thing Ed knew was that the two entities were walking away towards an object resembling an upturned water tank mounted on girder-like legs beside the canal. On the side was a peculiar red symbol. Although he insists that he never took his eyes off the men for a moment the two figures suddenly vanished into thin air. Then, the red mark on the side of the tank also vanished. Finally the object rose silently into the air, until, when at about rooftop height, it too simply disappeared in the blinking of an eye.

Ed waited for a few minutes to regain his composure and then decided to abandon his mundane task for the night. He picked up the machine and wheeled it back towards Cadishead, pausing under a street lamp to look at something odd that he now spotted on the seat.

Part of the seat had been ripped away and the petrol cap was missing from the bike. There was also a white powder scattered over the top. He got rid of most of this but thankfully retained a small sample which he put into a plastic bag and sent on to us for analysis.

The powder was nothing particularly out of this world. It had a magnesium and aluminium base, rather like the powder used by police to dust for fingerprints or contained in certain types of paint.

The motorcycle itself was quickly sold. Edward Dutton decided that it was more trouble than it was worth and could not face the prospect of having to fill out an insurance claim for the damage.

This is hardly a surprise. Could you find the right words to put onto a claim form, explaining how your motorbike was damaged by two church ministers from Mars who stepped out of a giant water tank parked by the Manchester Ship Canal?

3

MYSTERIOUS MANCHESTER

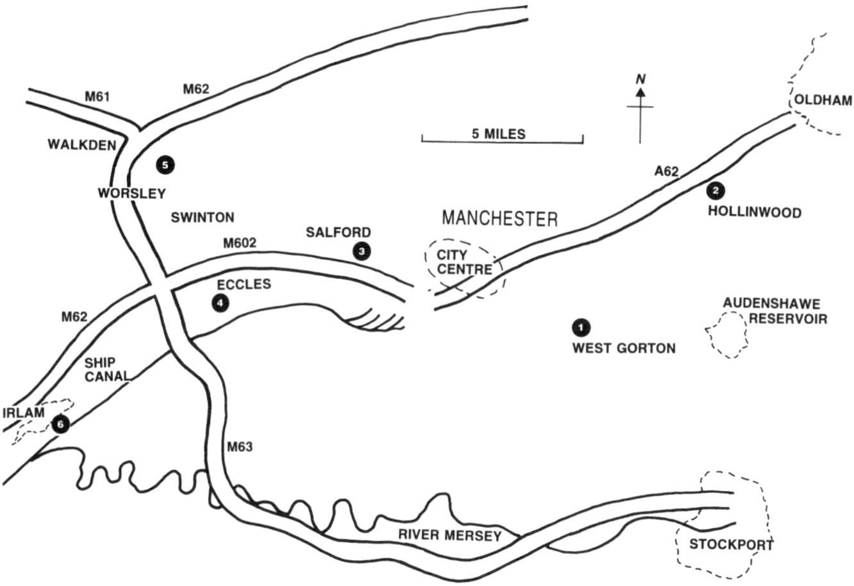

1.	Westgorton UFO Landing	2.	Hollinwood Ghost / Mummy
3.	Salford Poltergeist	4.	Eccles Poltergeist
5.	Wardley Hall Ghost	6.	Irlam Poltergeist

North and West Manchester

The River Mersey from its genesis in Stockport flirts with the bigger city of Manchester as it skirts Stretford and Urmston towards its temporary union with the famous Ship Canal. This area is awash with mystery and intrigue. But before we travel that far north, let us look at an incident recorded near Manchester International Airport.

The ghost of 613 Squadron

No one really knows what causes poltergeist activity to start up. Poltergeist is a German word meaning 'noisy spirit'. The main hallmarks of the poltergeist are the inexplicable sounds it generates and the movement of objects. Usually there is a 'focus' – sometimes, although not always, a young woman going through puberty. The theory is that pent up emotional energy exteriorises itself in a very physical manner. A more likely explanation however is that this 'energy' is seized on by an entity and used to power it in our world. When the energy source fades, so does the haunting.

Close to Manchester International Airport are the offices of a freight-forwarding company called Claridge & Co. The building was originally a barrack block for 613 Manchester Squadron of the RAF. An apparition and associated poltergeist activity were experienced by cleaners and clerical staff several times beginning in 1971. The apparition was of an old man, and witnesses included a lorry driver and a police officer.

The police were called out when loud screams and other noises were heard coming from the empty offices. No one was on the premises, but equipment had been moved. On the second occasion there were more screams plus the sound of footsteps. A company clerk described how he saw the figure of an old man sitting in the storeroom next to his office. He opened the adjoining door to ask who he was, but no one was there. Several nights later a number of other staff watched the old man walk through the office in bare feet.

The case of the crashed 'Russian helicopter'

Did an unidentified flying object land by the side of a block of flats in West Gorton sometime during the summer of 1968? That is the claim of a family who lived in Bennett Street in West Gorton. The flats have since been demolished, and it has been difficult to trace former residents to verify the story, but here it is.

Mr Patel* worked in an Indian restaurant in Manchester and did not finish until late at night. On this particular evening, Mr Patel's English wife, Diane*, was at home alone with their three young children. The two boys shared a room, and four-year old Gemma* had a bed in the same room as her parents. They were on the second floor, and the parents' bedroom overlooked a grassed area.

The children were asleep. It was around 11pm. Diane Patel crept into her bedroom so as not to disturb Gemma, as she needed to put some clothing away. Outside it was a warm summer's evening. She could hear the rowdy noise of other residents out on the balconies of the flats, when suddenly someone cried out in surprise. Thinking a fight had begun – not an uncommon occurrence – she went to the bedroom window to see what was happening. Mrs Patel received the shock of her life.

Coming slowly down at the side of the flats was a strange looking object. It was disc shaped and covered in a mass of coloured lights. Gemma remembers waking up and seeing the 'pretty lights' as they drew level with the window, and her mother pushing her back. Now Mrs Patel could see inside the object. Through a window she observed two figures dressed in ski suits. One of them was operating a lever. As the UFO touched down on the grass below, Diane Patel's memory ended, and she remembers nothing else until the following morning, when she took Gemma outside to the shops.

The grassed area was alive with activity. It had been cordoned off by police, and several men wearing what she described as 'bee keeping suits' were digging up the turf and removing it. When she asked a neighbour what had happened, he replied that a policeman had said that a secret Russian helicopter had crash-landed.

Mrs Patel had forgotten about the incident entirely, until a feature on UFOs shown on television several years later jolted her memory. Peter Hough had been alerted to the case by one of her sons, now grown up and married. David* felt there was something very wrong about that night which required investigation. Although he had no conscious memory of anything, he felt something nagging away at the back of his mind.

Under hypnosis, carried out by a psychologist in 1993, David described trying to hide under his bed when 'something' came into the room for him and his brother. As we have seen, hypnosis is sometimes used in cases when witnesses develop amnesia during a UFO encounter. It is used to take the witness back to the incident where – in theory at least – they relive the experience, including the 'hidden memory'. Although she had never previously been emotional about the sighting, Mrs Patel started weeping copiously when hypnosis was attempted on her. Whatever was buried in her unconscious mind seemed too painful even to contemplate.

Did the incident really happen? What about the other residents, and the police officers at the scene? How were the local press kept away from the story? Was the 'Russian helicopter' explanation used to keep everyone quiet? The authors would be pleased to hear from anyone who can shed some light on the case!

The Manchester mummy

In bygone times, many people were afraid of being buried alive. This fear was the product of real tragedy. Before the twentieth century medicine was rudimentary, and someone falling into a comatose state could be certified dead, condemned to a 'premature burial'. Edgar Allan Poe realised the horror in the classic story of that title written early in the nineteenth century.

Exhumed coffins from that period have shown scratch marks on the insides of coffin lids. At the time this was used to further the vampire legend, implying that the undead were active. The marks were probably the frantic efforts of wrongly buried victims trying to claw their way out. There are many cases on record where the tiny movement of an eye ball saved a 'corpse' from an early funeral.

In the middle of the eighteenth century, Madam Hannah Beswick of Birchen Bower House, Hollinwood, was all too aware of the possibility of premature burial. One of her own brothers was about to be buried when someone noticed signs of life. Several days later he was completely recovered. Madam Beswick was determined that the same fate would not befall her. She made a will in which all of her property was left to her doctor, providing he kept her remains above ground. Dr Charles White agreed to that and to a further clause which stipulated that every twenty-one years the body must be brought home to Birchen Bower and left there for a week.

When Madam Beswick finally died, Dr White embalmed her body with tar, then swathed it in bandages, leaving only the face uncovered. The mummy was kept at his home at Sale Priory. On at least one occasion the body was returned to Birchen Bower, where it was kept in the granary. During the week it was there, some very odd things happened with the livestock.

The locked doors of a stable and byre were discovered unaccountably open, with horses and cows missing. Some pigs and sheep which had also vanished were discovered several miles away, and a cow was found in a hayloft. It was all blamed on the troubled spirit of the old woman.

By this time Birchen Bower had been divided into workers' tenements. Several tenants described hearing the rustle of a silk dress, then the appearance of a figure described as that of Hannah Beswick. It was known that in 1745 the lady had hidden some gold in the building, fearing that Prince Charlie might reach Manchester and take her wealth. The gold was never found by her relatives.

Her ghost was often seen disappearing near a large flagstone in the parlour of a hand-loom weaver called 'Joe'. It was later discovered that Joe's sudden affluent life style was due to the fact he had lifted up the flagstone and discovered a tin containing gold wedges. He took this to Oliphants of Manchester and sold them. It was afterwards said that Madam Beswick's ghost took on a new and more sinister demeanour.

Witnesses claimed they had been confronted by a figure clad in a black silk gown and white cap, beams of harsh blue light emanating from her eyes, her posture one of anger and defiance. The granary glowed as if on fire, and strange noises were often heard.

The mummy was eventually moved from Sale Priory to a room belonging to the Manchester Natural History Society, where it was a source of much interest. As *The Manchester Guardian* reported on 15 August 1868, the remains were finally interned on 22 July in Harpurhey Cemetery. Even after Ferranti had built a factory on land formerly occupied by Birchen Bower, the apparition was still seen. And not only apparitions.

Nearby at Cairo Mill in 1972 a security guard was patrolling the grounds when he became aware of a humming sound. It was like a swarm of bees. Looking up he saw a strange object hovering at the side of the mill! The factory cat which also seemed to notice the object, ran away in terror and hid for several hours. John Byrne told BUFORA (British UFO Research Association) investigator Ron Drabble:

"I estimated it to be about one hundred feet in diameter because it seemed to completely fill the sky. The edge nearest to me was almost over the top of the bicycle shed. It also had what appeared to be rather a large window, in front of it. This was quite brightly lit with a bluey-white light."

John could not see anything through the 'window'. As he watched the object turned onto its edge revealing a definite saucer shape with a large domed top. Suddenly it shot straight up into the sky at a terrific speed and disappeared.

The Tully Street poltergeist

A poltergeist which attracted crowds of sightseers manifested in Tully Street, Salford in 1959.

The focus in this instance was the twelve-year-old son of the occupants. At one point the phenomenon seemed to be attempting to communicate through him, although the boy was indifferent. It started on Christmas Eve and continued almost without a break into February 1960. The noises consisted mainly of two types. One sounded like a heavy cannon ball bouncing across the ceiling, and the other a rhythmic pounding as if someone was using a sledgehammer. These noises were not subjective. They were so loud neighbours in the same row of houses reported hearing them too. The Rev. Edward Dimond, vicar of St. James's Church, Broughton, visited the house and heard them for himself.

In an attempt to discover a rational explanation, the premises were examined by police officials and engineers from the Water Board, the Gas Board and the Town Hall. No natural explanation was forthcoming. Scientists from Manchester University examined the house and studied the sounds which were not random, and seemed to exhibit a code of sorts.

The case attracted the attention of the media, which resulted in large numbers of people regularly gathering outside in Tully Street. Rev. Dimond was convinced the phenomena were caused by a resentful spirit who was trapped in the earth plane, unable to travel on into the afterlife.

With permission from the Bishop of Manchester, a service of exorcism was arranged in the house.

News of this spread, and on the day of the exorcism the crowds outside were so huge that the police had to be called in to disperse them. The service lasted half an hour, but it had the desired effect. There were no further manifestations – the entity was successfully sent on its way.

A similar case occurred in Eccles in the 1930s. A family lived peaceably for almost three years in a house on Liverpool Road. Then bedlam broke out. Inexplicable noises were heard from an upstairs room. The noises would continue throughout the night, and in the morning the family would discover that their beds had been moved. Members of the family also reported seeing, mainly on the ground floor, a dark figure dressed as a priest. On one occasion it was seen to disappear through a wall.

The family discovered that a former priest of St Mary's Church called Father Sharrock had died in the house at the turn of the century. Had something stirred the priest's spirit into activity? Prayers were said for Father Sharrock but things only became worse. Finally an exorcism was carried out by the then current incumbent of St Mary's, and the phenomenon stopped.

Murder through the mists of time

Wardley Hall was erected in Worsley by Thurston Tyldesley in Tudor times. This half timbered and moated house was later purchased by a family called Downes. Most notorious of them was a hell raiser called Roger Downes, the last of the male line, described as the 'most licentious of the courtiers of Charles II'.

After an evening's dissipation he staggered across London Bridge vowing to kill the first person he met. That person happened to be a poor tailor on his way home. The murder was witnessed by a watchman who raised his bill and struck off Roger's head, then heaved the body over the parapet into the Thames. His head was allegedly salvaged and returned to Wardley Hall around 1676.

Legends have been recorded about the skull which was kept in an embrasure between the staircase and the hall. These bare a remarkable resemblance to stories connected with other skulls kept in old houses around the country. At Wardley Hall it was said that the skull was tossed into the moat when a maidservant mistook it for an animal's. A sudden terrifying storm assailed the building, and the object was retrieved and returned to its niche. Every time the exhibit was disturbed, similar calamities befell the household.

As with most legends, on closer inspection things are not what they seem. When the Downes family vault was opened in Wigan Church in 1929, Roger was discovered with his skeleton intact. The top of his cranium had been sawn off, probably during a post mortem examination. Whose skull was it then that resided at Wardley Hall? Was it the head of a martyred priest? That is where the evidence points.

Ambrose Barlow was a Roman Catholic priest and a friend of the Downes family. He lived at Barlow Hall, Chorlton-cum-Hardy, which in modern times was converted into a golf club. He was convicted and executed at Lancaster in 1641, and his severed head was impaled on the tower of Collegiate Church in Manchester. Francis Downes eventually recovered it and took it to Wardley Hall. Strands of chestnut-coloured hair, which adhered to the skull for many years, were the same shade as those belonging to Father Barlow.

Worsley was also host for a time to the Tudor scholar and magician, Dr John Dee. Dee was born of Welsh parentage in London on 13 July 1527. Between 1542 and 1545 he studied at St John's College, Cambridge. Later he distinguished himself in mathematics, astronomy and, less-favourably, occultism.

There is no doubt that Dr Dee saw occultism as a legitimate study alongside astronomy and mathematics. This was particularly dangerous at a time when witch hunts across Europe had put to death thousands – probably millions – of alleged occultists. In 1555, he was put in prison for a short time on suspicion of casting enchantments against Queen Mary. Dee successfully cast a horoscope which correctly predicted the date of the coronation of Elizabeth I in 1558.

For many years he got a bad press from modern historians who largely ignored his contributions which in the sixteenth century earned him a reputation as the most learned man in Europe. In 1582 an abortive attempt was made by him to introduce the Gregorian Calendar into Britain. It was that same year that Dee formed a friendship with an occultist named Edward Kelly. Kelly allegedly had the power of necromancy. He brought a corpse to life in the St Leonard's Churchyard at

Walton-le-Dale, and for a time convinced Dee that a spirit had ordered the two men to swop wives.

It was in 1589 that Dr Dee came to Manchester where Queen Elizabeth made him Warden of Christ's College – a post he held for seven years. During that time he took up residence at Kempnough Hall, Worsley, where he left, according to tradition, an atmosphere of evil. A subsequent tenant called Sam Derbyshire, went berserk for no apparent reason. He hacked his wife to death, then slit the throat of his son. Some years later, a new tenant invited her daughter and grand daughter to stay at Kempnough Hall. The grandmother, who was very old, asked the little girl what she should leave her in her will. The child replied that she would like the crucifix hanging over grannie's bed. The grandmother was perplexed. There was no crucifix over the bed. Some months later the child ran downstairs in an excited state. She told the two women that she had entered her grandmother's bedroom, and had seen an angel on the mattress praying.

Was this a spiritual guardian of Kempnough Hall?

One autumn in the mid 1960s Mrs Dorothy Millington visited her daughter who lived in Worsley. It was a warm Sunday afternoon so they decided to take the dog and go out for a drive. Their journey took them down Hardy Lane in Chorlton-cum-Hardy – to a location we encountered in Chapter 2. After passing some tennis courts they parked the car and crossed Jackson's Bridge over the River Mersey.

They strolled across open marshland filled with people similarly enjoying the fine weather. Suddenly, to Mrs Millington's perceptions, the day turned damp and foggy. As she later explained to paranormal investigator Terence Whittaker:

"I got a horrid feeling of misery and depression, but strangely enough, no one around me seemed to be bothered, or, as you would expect, begin to make for home."

Close by is the sewage treatment plant enclosed by concrete buttresses. The dog ran towards this then stopped abruptly, as if sensing something. It came back with its tale between its legs obviously frightened. At this point Mrs Millington noticed the pathetic figure of a child standing near the plant. It was a small scrawny boy wearing school clothes and a raincoat more suited to the 1930s. The woman thought he looked anxious and miserable as he looked at her and spoke.

"The man's name is George Ware", he said.

The sewage treatment plant on marshland near Chorlton-cum-Hardy. Mrs Millington saw the figure of a schoolboy in 1930s dress standing by the concrete buttresses; did he give her the name of his murderer? (Peter Hough)

The depressing fog went, and with it the boy.

The story would have ended there, just another meaningless psychic experience, but during his investigations Terence Whittaker uncovered some startling information.

One night in the mid 1930s a black fog descended over Manchester. Despite the pleas of his mother, her eleven-year old son insisted on leaving the house to keep a mysterious rendezvous. The boy did not get on well at home and was described as very secretive. A tram crew remembered dropping the boy off after their efforts to dissuade him from going out into the fog failed. They watched him meet an older young man who put his arm around the boy as they walked off in the direction of Hardy Lane.

The following day after the fog had dispersed, the boy's body was discovered at the sewage works. His throat had been cut with a razor. Because of the homosexual overtones the murder was hardly mentioned in the press, and despite the police investigation no one was charged with the crime.

Had Mrs Millington been given the name of the murderer by his victim? Did a 'George Ware' live in the Chorlton area? If so, this is a remarkable case. It goes a long way to suggesting that we do indeed survive physical death. Does any reader have any information on this case?

Happenings at Irlam

Irlam sits beside the canal stretch of the River Mersey. A near miracle feat of engineering in its day, the Manchester Ship Canal has little commercial use now, although the leisure industry is set to restore life into its neglected banks and waters. But whatever man does, it will make no difference to the legions of the mysterious who haunt, and will continue to haunt, the lives of the people of the Mersey Valley.

It has long been understood that poltergeists know no class distinction. The phenomenon is not fickle. A two bedroomed semi is just as suitable a place to wreak havoc as a stately home. Council houses in particular come in for their share of attention. Frank and Julie Owen were at the end of their tether in June 1989 when the *Manchester Evening News* reported on the story.

They lived in a twenty-year old council house situated on Peregrine Drive. The phenomena started around nine months before. It began with the couple's three-year old daughter, Joanne. She told her parents that an old woman had often appeared and had talked and played games with her. The Owens dismissed it as imagination, as many young children invent playmates – although these are usually children like themselves. Then other things started happening.

The television set switched itself off, an alarm clock was smashed, the 'old lady' began swearing at Joanne, and mysterious knocks were heard on internal doors. When the family called in a medium, a door lock was thrown at this person. One night, things became so frightening the Owens left the house and stayed with relatives. But the knocking sounds were not confined to their house. Tony and Sharon Maunder who lived in the adjoining property recorded their experiences.

Mr Maunder described how he was taking a bath when he heard someone knocking on the door. When he opened it, no one was there.

The same thing happened when his wife was having a bath. This was before they knew what was happening next door.

In a final desperate attempt, Father Lionel Devany of St Joseph's Church agreed to help the family and blessed the house.

4

TALES OF THE NORTH CHESHIRE PLAINS

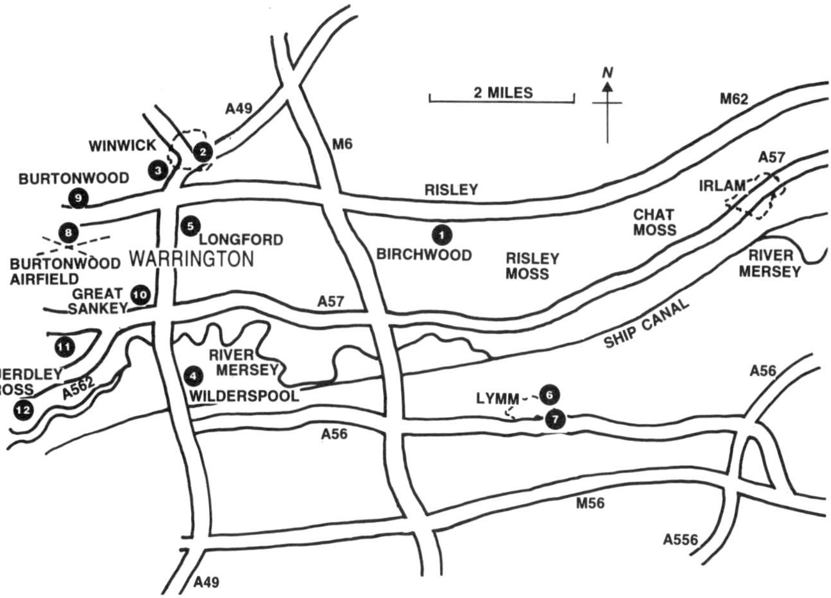

1.	Risley Entity	2.	Winwick Demon Pig
3.	Winwick Ghost / Soldier	4.	Wildrespool Ghost Cavalier
5.	Longford Poltergeist	6.	Lymm Ball of Fire
7.	Lymm Phantom Aircraft	8.	Burtonwood Airfield Ghosts
9.	Burtonwood Motorway UFO	10.	Warrington UFO
11.	Great Sankey Phantom Brick	12.	Cuerdley / Bold Dragon

The area in and around Warrington

The A57 runs alongside the Manchester Ship Canal from Irlam right into the centre of the market town of Warrington. But first we must look to the north.

Three miles to the east of Warrington lies the Birchwood housing estate. The development, with its modern shopping and leisure centre, is an established feature of the area, nudging close to the Risley Moss nature reserve. But in 1978 there was nothing. On this vast tract of land, currently providing the habitat for a 20,000 population, clung the broken derelict remains of another time.

During the last World War, the entire area was a huge munitions dump. Until the arrival of the housing development, its concrete bunkers and rusted wrought iron buildings were still visible, weed choked and long abandoned. Signs proclaiming: MINISTRY OF DEFENCE – KEEP OUT, were visible from the nearby main Culcheth to Warrington road.

In February 1947, the Ministry of Supply took over a small part of the area and developed the U. K. Atomic Energy Authority complex, comprising offices and laboratories. The UKAEA installation bordered Daten Avenue – a service road which connected with the nearby M62 motorway. Also close by Daten Avenue, on the opposite side, were an A.A. Relay Station, and a university research building. It was a quiet, lonely road, but one Ken Edwards knew very well . . .

Ken, tall and gangly, was a very affable man in his late thirties. He was a service engineer who lived with his wife, Barbara, in a bungalow in Fearnhead, near Risley. On March 17th, 1978 – St Patrick's Day – Ken had been to work as usual, arrived home, washed and changed, then rushed out again to attend a trade union meeting in Sale.

The meeting was routine. He had drunk little, having to face the forty-minute drive home afterwards. The motorway shone darkly in the headlights of Ken's van as the wide petrified river of tarmac flowed alongside the unspoilt wastes of Chat Moss. 'The Moss', as local people call it, is ten miles of desolate peat bog lying between Manchester and Warrington.

About a mile and a half from home, he slowed down, indicated, and left the motorway at Risley via an unsign-posted slip road. This was used mainly by maintenance vehicles, but provided a handy short cut for local people. He had left the meeting at 11pm. He glanced at his watch and saw it was now approaching 11.30pm.

The van rattled along the road. There were no other vehicles. The total darkness was eerie. Ken knew that beyond the glare of the headlights huddled the twisted skeletons of long abandoned World War Two ordnance factories. A generation before, hundreds of people had toiled there with the machineries of death.

As he approached the A.A. Relay Station, Ken changed down to negotiate a small island, before continuing slowly up Daten Avenue. He was just moments away from an event that was to change his life forever – perhaps with fatal consequences.

Ahead, to his right, was a grassy embankment skirted with bushes and small trees, beyond which lay the university building. On the left, just coming up, was a ten-foot high chain linked security fence surrounding land belonging to the UKAEA. On the embankment, the van headlights illuminated an impossible looking figure.

Ken stared goggle-eyed as his brain tried desperately to find a nice comfortable niche for the incongruity now only a small distance away. At the same time he slowed down the van until it was stationary at the side of the road. Ken tried to place the figure within the cosy framework of his day to day life. Could it be someone, anyone, a prankster perhaps – even at this late hour, climbing in such a peculiar fashion down the embankment? He watched, entranced, as the bizarre event unfolded.

As the thing walked down the steep embankment it held its arms out straight from the body like someone sleep-walking. Further to this, it was walking at right-angles to the ground – an impossible stance. Anyone walking down the slope would have to tilt their whole body backwards in order not to topple forwards. At last it reached the bottom and stood on the wide verge staring across the road. Now Ken had a much better view of it, and for the moment at least, it seemed oblivious of him, the van and its lights.

The thing was over seven-feet tall and covered almost entirely in silver. Its head was shaped like a goldfish bowl, coloured black, sitting on a broad body. But the most alarming feature was its arms. Like something from a nightmare they grew out of the top of its shoulders! Ken felt the panic rising from the pit of his stomach as he realised that the thing was real, and further more it was not human.

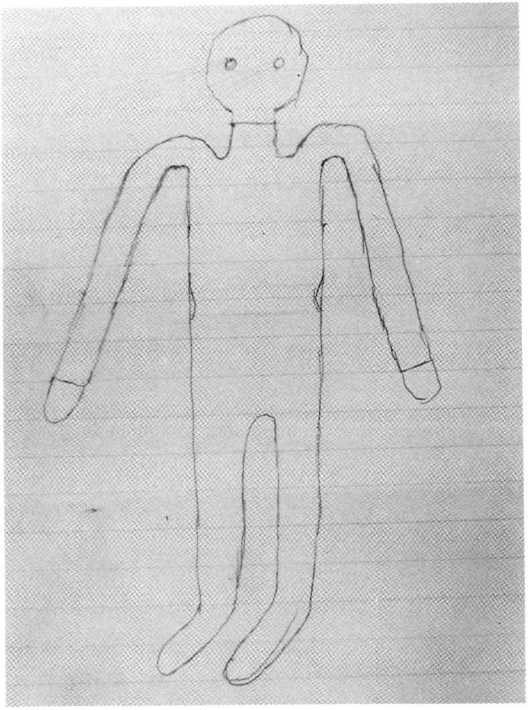

The drawing of the entity Ken made after his horrifying ordeal. (Jenny Randles)

Ken Edwards sat crouched in the seat, gripping the steering wheel, wishing fervently he could just disappear. There was no chance of that, no possibility of reversing and driving away, or of opening the car door and making a run for it. He seemed to be paralysed. Several days later, the bewildered man described to the authors the way he had felt.

"My head was swimming with strange thoughts. There were hundreds of them, all racing through my mind at once. I also felt very odd. It was a sensation like two enormous hands pressing down on me from the top. The pressure was tremendous. It seemed to paralyse me. I could only move my eyes. The rest of me was rigid."

Suddenly the figure was on the move again. It took a few steps to cross the road, but it seemed ill equipped for this most simple of manoeuvres. The entire body moved very stiffly, the legs articulating from the hips – no evidence of knee joints at all. Then it stopped, right in the middle of the highway. Ken knew he was not going to escape so lightly. The thing knew he was there. Slowly its head began to swivel, and for the first time he noticed it had eyes – or something which resembled eyes, set at the top of the head. From these 'eyes' projected two pencil-slim beams of light. They pierced the windscreen for about a minute, it seemed, pinning the man like a butterfly in a case. Then the head turned forward again, and the thing continued its laborious walk across the road and onto the verge opposite.

What would it do now? The high chain-linked fenced blocked its path. Would it turn right, or . . . The alternative started the panic again in his stomach. What would he do if it turned towards the van?

It did neither. Perhaps if it had, Ken would have been able to cope with it better. The thing walked up to the fence, raised its arms again, and walked right through it. It was as if the fence did not exist; as if, at the moment of contact, the atoms of the fence had become benign, changed their orientation, and allowed the entity to pass through unharmed. The entity shambled up the slope on the other side, swallowed by the darkness, in the direction of the moss.

With difficulty, Ken managed to get the van into gear. He retained only a vague memory of the short drive home. And there was further confusion. The experience had seemed to last just a few minutes, but it was 12.30am when he pulled up on the drive, a discrepancy of roughly three quarters on an hour!

He pushed his way into the house and uncharacteristically went straight to the drinks' cabinet. Barbara followed him into the lounge and watched as he gulped back a large whisky. She was already worried because of his late arrival, and now she was convinced something awful had occurred – a road accident perhaps. She asked him what had happened. The words tripped out, nonsense words, words that slammed into one another.

"I've seen a silver man", he said.

When he had calmed a little, he told her the whole story.

Barbara was flabbergasted. How could she believe such a story? The whole thing was insane. Yet, she knew her husband well. He was a straightforward, uncluttered sort of person, not one to tell lies, or tall stories. But above all it was obvious that something had happened. It was written on his face, and what was that curious burn mark, on the inside fingers of his right hand?

Ken Edwards started undressing for bed hoping that routine would anchor him back into the world of normality. It was useless. He had to tell someone, had to report it. Barbara looked aghast as he began dressing again.

"I think I'd better go to the police", he mumbled. "Will you take me?"

He huddled into the passenger seat during the short journey to Padgate police station. The officers on duty were not amused. At first they thought it was a St Patrick's Day prank. But they too quickly became convinced of his sincerity. Besides, the man was in a state. Crazy though the story was, they decided to mount an investigation immediately.

A call was put through to the UKAEA plant. A police car with two officers then followed the couple home. Barbara went inside while Ken climbed into the back of the car, before it continued its short journey to Daten Avenue. There waited a surprise. It was still the early hours of the morning. The darkness remained complete, giving the lonely road an eerie, expectant feel. There, straddling the width of the avenue, stood a large group of uniformed men.

There were about twenty-five, armed with batons and electric torches. They were security officers from the UKAEA, alerted by the police.

Ken climbed out of the car, and at the invitation of one of the policemen, nervously recounted what had happened just a short time before. Perhaps it was the atmosphere of the place, but there was no smirking nor derision from any of the men. Several of them fingered their batons and looked about warily. They examined the chain-linked fence but found it completely undamaged. Then a general search of the area on the other side of the road, where the entity had emerged, was made. When Ken pointed out he had last seen it heading towards some trees on the edge of the moss, none of the officers would volunteer to venture there in the dark and look. Finally, he was driven home. But this was not the end of the story – it was only the beginning. The end was to be much more devastating.

Within hours, the police had leaked the story to the press, and during most of Saturday, and much of the following week, Barbara and Ken Edwards were besieged by newsmen and weird religious cult members.

As all the fuss died down, he had time to think more deeply about what had happened. Several things worried him. Something was wrong with the time. He had left the union meeting at 11pm, and had come off the motorway about half an hour later. Normally he would have been home by 11.45pm at the latest. The experience only seemed to last a few minutes, so why did he arrive home at 12.30am – three-quarters of an hour after coming off the M62?

Did he just sit there for all that time, suffering from shock? As far as he knew, the van engine was left idling, yet it failed to show a large consumption of petrol. Could there be another answer, something with more sinister ramifications?

Although Ken Edwards did not know it, 'time-lapses' crop up in many cases where people have witnessed strange phenomena. Many of these victims, from all parts of the world, all different kinds of cultures, have been hypnotised by qualified psychiatrists and clinical psychologists, in attempts to 'fill in' the missing time. The scenario which emerges is nearly always the same.

The witness is abducted and taken into a featureless white room. There, he is made to lie down on a table where movement is impossible. The table is then surrounded by several grotesque looking beings who carry out physical and mental testing on their captive. Finally the witness finds himself back behind the wheel of his car, with no conscious memory of what occurred during the missing time . . .

Would a similar 'memory' have emerged if Ken Edwards had been hypnotised? His watch had stopped at 11.45 – several minutes after the onset of the experience. Because of subsequent events, we shall never know.

However, there were other, more tangible indications of the reality of the experience. On the Monday morning when Ken drove to work, he tried to use his radio transceiver but it failed to operate. Company electricians took the machine apart and were mystified. An enormous power surge – possibly through the aerial – had burned out the entire transmitting diode circuit. Most of the capacitors in the circuit were also destroyed. Because of the enormous cost of repair, it was decided to scrap the unit and fit a new one.

Then there were the burns – similar to sunburn – which marked several fingers of his right hand; the hand which gripped the steering wheel when the entity aimed the beams of light into the vehicle. If there was a connection, then what kind of energy could burn out a radio transceiver and effect the skin in this way?

So what had this amiable service engineer experienced on St Patrick's Day, 1978?

There were two theories which would explain the incident, partly at least, in mundane terms. Rumours of a stunt by a nearby local college were investigated by the police, as P. C. Roy Kirkpatrick, explained to the authors.

"The college did get up to stunts back then, you know, stealing wheels from cars and so on. But we looked into the idea. There was no Rag on at the time and nobody ever admitted it. We never could find evidence for such a link."

Ken Edwards was unimpressed by the rumours too.

"I wish he or she would come forward and tell me how they did it . . . How they blew up my radio and walked through the fence! It was some stunt!"

Could it have been a fireman in a silver foil radiation suit attached to the UKAEA complex?

The police, with staff at the UKAEA, arranged a little subterfuge. Officers called at Ken's house, and asked him to accompany them back to the nuclear research plant for further questioning. At a pre-arranged signal, one of the staff wearing a fireman's suit, strode out in front of the car. The officers carefully watched Ken's reaction.

"That was what you saw – wasn't it?"

Ken never batted an eye lid.

"Nope! Nothing like it", he told them.

If there is a paranormal answer, then are there any clues regarding its source?

The village of Risley was founded by Thomas Risley, and the church he built was one of the oldest Presbyterian buildings in England. When the M62 scythed through the area, the church was swept out of its way. The grave yard remains, just a short distance from Daten Avenue. Did the church lie on a ley? Could a violent disruption of the ley caused by the arrival of the motorway, with all its attendant noise and pollution, cause 'things' to happen?

In 1987, the authors uncovered some other very interesting factors. The university building on that side of Daten Avenue where the entity appeared, is jointly owned by Liverpool University, and the University of Manchester. There is a small nuclear reactor in this building – hence the radiation suits across the road at the UKAEA, but more interesting are the experiments carried out in a sensory deprivation unit.

The idea of these units is to totally isolate a human being from all exterior stimuli for long periods of time. During these experiments, participants have reported very vivid mystical and hallucinatory

The idea of these units is to totally isolate a human being from all exterior stimuli for long periods of time. During these experiments, participants have reported very vivid mystical and hallucinatory experiences. Occasionally angelic or demonic beings are conjured up. Are these from the inner space of the mind, or from some exterior source? Was there an experiment underway on the night of March 17th, 1978? Could Ken Edwards have been witnessing someone else's nightmare?

Certainly there is a strong belief in the East that certain priests can create 'thought forms' called 'tulpas'; the entities, created in the mind of the priest, might take on a life of their own for a short period. The act of meditation in isolated mountain caves and temples is not dissimilar to modern experiments in isolation units.

Ken Edwards was to see the entity one more time. On 23 March a UFO investigator from Leeds came down to see him. Ken agreed to visit the site. Once there, Ken began to feel dizzy. From the corner of his eye he momentarily saw the entity. It was visible for just a few moments.

Things did not go well with Ken Edwards. Less than a year after the encounter he began to feel lethargic and suffered stomach cramps. A specialist diagnosed cancer of the kidneys. In early 1980 he underwent emergency surgery, and it seemed to be successful. But a few months later he developed cancer of the throat, and in 1982, aged just forty-two, Ken Edwards died.

It would be circumstantial to link his premature death with the strange experience. Although, as Barbara pointed out: here was a phenomenon which could stop a watch, cause burns and destroy a radio transceiver. What might such energy do to the long-term health of a human being?

The demon pig of Winwick

The small community of Winwick lies to the north of Warrington on the A49 where St Oswald's Church is not without its mystery. It was built on an ancient burial mound which lies on a ley stretching from a Bronze Age mound on Winter Hill, across into Cheshire. Pagan temples and artifacts were deliberately placed on leys where they could, in theory, tap into this 'energy'. Subsequently, the Christians built on top of these.

There is a story that the church was originally under construction at a different site. At that time there was a demon terrorising the area in the shape of a wild boar. The demon objected to the church being built away from the ley. Each night, after the masons had gone home, the stones were removed and discovered the following morning on the pagan burial mound.

Eventually, the builders gave in to the demon pig, and the church was constructed in its present position not far from the sacred well of St Oswald.

Oswald was King of Northumbria, killed in battle with Penda, King of Mercia on 5 August 642 at Winwick. The place where he fell soon attracted souvenir hunters. They removed the sods where his body had lain. Water began to flow at the spot which was discovered to possess special healing properties. The name of Winwick is said to have come about after the squeal of the pig: Ween-ick! Ween-ick! The demon was subsequently subdued by the Christians, and this is symbolised in a carving set in the church wall above the west entrance. It shows a pig tethered to a block of stone.

St Oswald's Church, Winwick, a pig is carved in the stone work to commemorate the the demon pig that terrorised the stone masons. (Peter Hough)

A ghostly legacy

There are many old legends and mysteries associated with Warrington. Built on the banks of the River Mersey, the town supported the Roundheads during the Civil War, and boasts one of only five statues ever cast of Oliver Cromwell. This is situated at the bottom of Bridge Street, just yards from the famous river.

The imposing statue of Oliver Cromwell just yards from the Mersey at Bridge Foot.. (Peter Hough)

During the civil war a battle took place near Winwick Hospital where hundreds of men were killed. Perhaps then, it is not surprising that there have been several ghostly sightings of Cromwellian soldiers in the area.

In 1925, the Coach & Horses public house at Sankey organised a day trip to Blackpool. On its return, the coach stopped near Winwick for some of its occupants to relieve themselves in a nearby field. Imagine their embarrassment turning quickly to fear as they were confronted by the figures of a dozen or so 17th century Cromwellian Ironsides!

A car containing several Widnes rugby supporters was travelling home from Wigan in 1949, when it suffered a puncture. The car pulled in at the side of the road on its approach to Winwick and the men climbed out to change the tyre. In the mist covering a field, they were astounded to see three Cromwellian soldiers. The figures were not the least bit ethereal, but looked perfectly real. This is a feature in most ghost sightings. The men observed them for about half an hour, then shot off home in the car.

On the south bank of the Mersey in Wilderspool is the legend of a ghostly Cavalier. He was most active during the 19th century, when many people from various backgrounds reported seeing him sitting on the river bank, and at several locations between Bridge Foot and Appleton.

Local author Wally Barnes related the story told to him in 1958 by a former police officer. Apparently, in 1934 the officer had been approached by a lady in the Blue Bell Dingle area, who reported that her puppy had gone missing. He went to search the Dingle and saw a man, whom, he thought, was wearing fancy dress. The man was adorned in the splendour of a Cavalier.

The officer approached him, truncheon drawn, sensing something was not right. Suddenly he realised he could see through the figure, which slowly faded away. Wally Barnes discovered that a battle had been fought at Bridge Foot, and the defeated Royalists had fled into some local woods. Many died that day. Was the Cavalier one of them?

A modern case of haunting occurred in the Longford district of Warrington from 1989 until 1991. It was a classic poltergeist manifestation that plagued a family who had bought their council house. All six members of the family plus their friends experienced the phenomena.

One visitor leapt from a chair when he felt a cold hand on his back. No one was near him. Electrical equipment kept breaking down causing the family to buy four freezer units, two television sets and a replacement washing machine – all within twelve months! Clothing was moved around in rooms protected with child proof locks. The mother commented to the *Manchester Evening News*:

"The unusual sequence of events is very worrying. At first, my husband was sceptical. Then his dinner suddenly went missing and the plate was found in a locked bedroom. Small items keep disappearing and reappearing without explanation."

Was the phenomenon caused by the mischievous spirit of a little girl? On several occasions Rebel, the family's Alsatian was seen barking at an unseen presence. Their ten-year old daughter was frightened by the shadowy figure of a young girl. The mother added:

"Neighbours told us that a little girl died in the house forty years ago. My eldest daughter says she has seen this girl laughing at her. There are too many strange happenings for us not to take them seriously."

Future mysteries

Top science fiction author Bob Shaw, made his home near Warrington several years ago. He left Belfast for England in 1973 'to escape the madness'. It is ironic and sad that two children should be murdered and many people injured by the IRA on the streets of his adopted town in March 1993.

Bob's first novel, *Night Walk,* was published in 1967. It has since been followed by twenty-eight more novels and short story collections. His fiction has appeared around the world including South America, Germany and Russia and he has won two Hugos – top awards.

Science Fiction is primarily about ideas. *Light of Other Days* explores the notion of 'slow glass'. Bob's literary invention postulates a glass which slows down the passage of light. Imagine, as Bob does, watching a scene through a window which actually took place years ago – things, people, who are no more.

His *Orbitsville* trilogy became a science fiction classic when the first volume was published in 1975. More recently saw the publication of another inventive trilogy. *The Ragged Astronauts* kicks off the tale of a medieval culture set on binary worlds a few thousand miles apart linked by a common atmosphere. Bob had a set-back in 1991 when he suffered a personal tragedy, but he recovered his place two years later with two new books. One is for budding authors entitled *How to Write Science Fiction,* and the other is a humorous novel called *Warren Peace.*

Some of his books deal with paranormal premises. In *Fire Pattern* for instance he explores the alleged phenomenon of spontaneous human combustion. The authors of this book investigated the case of a student who burst into flames on the stairs of a college in Widnes, on 28 January 1985. The inquest conclusion that the cause was a gas cooker was challenged by many, including senior fire officers.

Peter Hough asked Bob Shaw to pin-point the attraction of Science Fiction.

"From Stone Age man we have looked up at the starlit sky with a sense of wonder. Now we know the stars are distant suns, many of them with their own planetary systems, some of which must harbour intelligent life. Anyone with a bit of imagination must have visualised these alien worlds and wondered what they looked like. But more intriguing than the worlds are their inhabitants. A world able to sustain life wouldn't be all that different from our own, but the aliens could be totally different."

The Lymm lights

Just before we continue westwards, it is worth taking a diversion along the A56 south of the river to the Cheshire village of Lymm. The village is typical of many once-small communities situated too near burgeoning towns and cities. At its heart is a hotch potch of pubs and village shops set around a cobbled area called The Cross where historically local yobs were confined in the stocks. On its periphery however Philistine developers have wreaked their chaos with several housing estates. Despite all this, the Bridgewater canal, winding through the village centre, adds to its central beauty. Lymm has its share of legends. One tells of an old woman who found it more convenient to fill her pail from the church spout instead of the well as her neighbours did. One day she was drawing water as usual when a long bony hand shot out of the spout and knocked the pail away. The frightening experience taught the old woman a lesson.

Several modern mysteries concern us now.

A young man called Alex* was driving through the village on his way home to Altrincham on 3 December 1977. It was around 7.30pm as he passed along Rush Green Road. He noticed on the pavement ahead of him a boy riding a skate board. As he drove by Alex glanced in his wing mirror, and was astounded to see several orange glowing rings surrounding the boy. They were about six inches above the pavement and seemed to be wobbling. Alex told Peter Hough they had the brightness of an electric fire. Yet they had not been visible on his approach, and the boy seemed oblivious to the phenomenon.

Only seven days earlier, Alex experienced another light phenomenon while at work in Warrington. Alex worked for a menswear retailer on Horse Market Street. The shop was quiet at the time due in part to a storm which was raging outside. He was standing by the side of the office when he noticed a pear shaped light enter through the back window, wiggle across the shop floor before disappearing through the locked side door. It happened too quickly for him to alert anyone else until it was too late. Were the phenomena connected? If not, was the second an example of ball lightning, generated by the electric storm?

Earlier that year, around May, Gerry Mitchell was driving on the outskirts of Lymm when he experienced an inexplicable need to pull over to the side of the road. He just knew something was going to happen. As the feeling intensified, he wound down the window. There was an aura of strangeness. He felt isolated. The silence was uncanny and there were no other vehicles on the road. Suddenly, a line of three fluorescent green spheres whizzed silently past. Only after they had gone did things return to normal.

When Jenny Randles talked to Gerry Mitchell she told him that another witness had described the feeling 'like being suddenly at the bottom of a very deep well'. He thought this was very apt.

As a schoolboy, Peter Hough lived in the village and had his own strange encounter. It happened on the coat tail of a nationwide flap of sightings of 'flying crosses'. In one case, two police officers chased an object for several miles as it flew at tree-top height. While Peter's lacked the drama of this, it was just as intriguing.

"I remember it vividly to this day. It was the 8th October 1968, and I was fourteen and a half years old. I earned my pocket money by doing a newspaper round for Baker's Newsagents on Booths Hill. When the weather was good I enjoyed my job, and that particular autumnal morning was beautiful dry and crisp. The last thing on my mind was unidentified flying objects! If anything, my thoughts were turned to a day of maths and physics, which I didn't relish.

"I started my round at about 7.15am. It included Eagle Brow, an old area of the village containing several large detached houses with extensive gardens. One of my customers was a Dr Bateson* who lived in a place called Four Ways because it had four access points. The doctor, hearing the tyres of my bicycle crunch on the gravel drive, usually met me on the porch steps wearing his dressing gown. Then we would exchange a cheery 'good morning' and I would hand over a large bundle of newspapers. On this particular morning he did not appear.

"As usual, I steered my bicycle onto the steep gravel drive and pedalled through the twilight – made gloomier by the trees and bushes pressing in on either side. The drive opened out where it met the house, elevated above the quiet road. I stopped, and when the doctor did not appear, prepared to dismount, but something arrested my attention.

"Autumn was early that year, and already most of the trees were stripped bare. I saw what I took to be a crudely executed model aircraft caught in the branches of a tree. It was perfectly still and at an obtuse angle. Thinking no more, I climbed off the bike and placed Dr Bateson's newspapers in the porch. As I was getting back on the bike, the object caught my attention again, and I realised my first conclusions about it had been a trick of perception. It was, in fact, a large object about half a mile behind the tree. I knew this because it was now slowly righting itself into a horizontal position.

"Although it was still dusky at ground level, the clear sky was flooding with light. This perfectly silhouetted the object enabling me to accurately assess its shape. No wonder I had been fooled into thinking it was a toy! Although it was about the size of a passenger aircraft, it lacked any streamlining and was perfectly quiet. The fuselage was blunt at both ends, there was no tail fin, and the 'wings' were stubby rectangles which protruded from the exact centre of the object. Along the fuselage, just above the wings, were two rows of white lights which flashed like the fairy lights on a Christmas tree.

"As I struggled to place this phenomenon into my existing mind set, it began to move off very slowly until it was temporarily obscured from view by a thicket. Seconds later it reappeared much higher in the sky. This led me to conclude that the object had risen vertically. It now continued its silent flight, stopping and starting again. Suddenly it changed direction. Not by flying in a broad arc, but by turning on its axis. I watched as it drifted out of sight in the direction of Manchester."

Many years later, while Peter was guesting on a local radio show, a listener called in to report that he too had seen the same object over Lymm at that time. Was there a rational explanation, or could the object have originated from elsewhere?

The haunted airbase

The old Burtonwood airbase is situated just to the west of Warrington, bisected by the M62 which runs between Manchester and Liverpool. It was a thriving military centre during World War Two, but now is staffed only by a token RAF contingent. There are several ghostly stories associated with the base.

Late Christmas Eve, 1946, two American NCOs were returning to their billet after celebrating at The Rose Hotel on Hood Lane when they saw ahead of them a strange-looking mist, similar to a puff of smoke. As they drew nearer, the mist resolved itself into the figure of an airman – complete except for a missing head. This apparition was reported again by a boilerman and a group of women returning from a dance. Later, the Headless Airman was seen near Bewsey Old Hall and Crosfield Recreation Ground.

Speculation was rife as to the ghost's identity. Someone connected the sightings with a tragic event in 1944, when a bomber crash landed at the base and the pilot pressed his ejector button by mistake. His head was sliced off on the half open turret. Today, Burtonwood's giant aircraft hangers are used mainly for storage, and one in particular, hanger 'K', is a museum.

Englishman, Mike Meadows* gave up his Saturdays to work in the museum renovating military aircraft. During one afternoon is 1978 he was alone working on an amphibious type. At the bottom of the hanger stood a bus, rescued from a wood. Apparently it was one of the first buses put into service locally. As Mike worked on the aircraft, a creeping sensation came over him. Looking up he noticed an old bearded man seated behind the wheel of the bus. He was about to walk down to the vehicle when his attention was diverted by the entrance of another museum member.

"Who let the old guy in?", Mike asked

"What old guy? There's only you and me here", came the bemused reply. They searched the hanger but the old man had gone.

The museum traced the bus back to an old lady. She said her brother, a gamekeeper, and something of a recluse, took to living in the dilapidated bus where it had been dumped, among the trees on the land where he worked. Someone brought Mike a photograph of the old timer who had died some years previously. Mike recognised him as the figure he had seen in hanger 'K'. The gamekeeper had made his kitchen in what was formerly the cab of the bus.

That is not the only odd experience encountered by Mike Meadows at the airbase. As he told Peter Hough, on this second occasion he was left feeling afraid and shaken.

Mike had worked hard all day in the museum, and left for home at 11.30pm. As he drove past gate '13', he noticed someone standing there. Surprisingly the man wore a military uniform in the fashion of World War Two. Mulling this over, Mike drove on, but then felt 'something' in the car beside him. The temperature dropped, and a glow manifested in the area of the passenger seat.

Normally he drove past the Burtonwood motorway service station, but this time, without really thinking why, he drove onto the car park and stopped. Then he did something that to this day he cannot explain. He walked around the front of the car to the other side, and opened the passenger door as if to let someone out . . .

There are other phenomena associated with the base too. In January 1978 at approximately 11.30pm, two police officers, Peter Lowe and Gareth Roberts, were patrolling the M62 travelling from Liverpool towards Warrington. As they neared the section that cuts the former airbase in half, they were astonished to see a blue, glowing object hovering over Bold Power Station to their left.

The object resembled a three-pointed star, like an inverted 'T'. Suddenly it rose and travelled right over the base and then hovered over Fiddlers Ferry Power Station to the right. Suddenly it began to pulsate before streaking upwards until it was out of sight. An independent witness said there were about thirty vehicles parked up on the hard shoulder watching the spectacle.

Later that same year, at 2am on 13 May, a Mr Bibby and his friend, Mr Hassall, were walking through Burtonwood when they noticed a flash of light in the sky in the direction of St Helens. The sky was very bright and clear that night. They thought no more of it until they were near the library. At this point both men watched a large orange ball hovering right over Burtonwood Airbase. After about half a minute, the object began to move away in an easterly direction until it was lost from sight behind some houses.

Warrington itself is not without its UFO sightings. Night shift worker, Alan Woods, went to close the factory doors at Peter Stubbs on 5 July 1989 when something caught his attention. 'It was a beautiful, cool, clear night. I don't remember seeing a night so clear. I stood looking up at the stars. Suddenly an object appeared. My immediate thought turned to the possibility of a kite, as it was triangular and completely silent. Then I thought: "I don't believe it!". It obviously was not a kite. The two forward sides were lined with dull orange lights or jets.

"There was a road not far away, with no traffic on it. The night was so completely still and quiet. At first, the object was travelling west to east, and then changed course southwards until it was lost from view over the roof tops. It didn't change course gradually, like an aircraft, but the point of the triangle turned abruptly. I knew it was solid, because when it passed overhead it blocked out the stars."

Joyce Blackburn was putting the empty milk bottles out on the doorstep when she noticed a brilliant pulsating white light in the sky. It was 10.45pm on Saturday, 28 October 1978. When the light did not move she called her husband who came outside with their two teenage children. Intrigued, they went and fetched a telescope and binoculars. When Mr Blackburn looked at the brilliantly lit object through the binoculars he had to turn away, as the object was too bright. Then slowly, it began moving towards them.

At one point the light 'went out', then came on again as it drew nearer. The large light went off again, but this time was replaced by several smaller ones. These comprised a white 'dome' light, and three red ones set underneath the object in a triangular configuration. By now it was passing directly overhead. They all very clearly observed its disc shape and domed top. Until then the object had been silent, but now, as it passed over, they heard a humming sound. It disappeared in the direction of Fiddlers Ferry Power Station – a favourite attraction it seems for UFOs!

A warning of murder

1976 was a memorable year. It was the year of The Drought. Rain was so scarce that hundreds of acres of grass and woodland went up in flames, and rivers and whole reservoirs lost millions of gallons of water. The River Mersey was at its lowest level in living memory. There was much to remember about 1976, but Gail Kegan* remembers it for none of these things. She remembers it because it was the year she was almost murdered.

Seventeen-year-old Gail and her mother worked at a bakery in Warrington. The family lived on a new housing estate in Great Sankey which was well within walking distance of their place of employment.

September arrived, and Mrs Kegan and her daughter were going to work as usual. It was an early start, and they left the house just after 5.30am. At the top of the estate they followed a short cut along a dirt track, where some houses were still being built. As they drew level with a bungalow, she later told the authors, something very strange occurred.

Along the front of the bungalow was a brick wall, and at the top of a short drive, a garage was under construction. It was dark. The two women were talking to one another when Gail stopped. There was a voice, and it was calling her name.

". . . G a i l . . . G a i l . . ." It seemed so clear, so definite.

"Did you hear that, mother?"

Mrs Kegan stopped and looked at her daughter, quizzically.

"Hear what?"

"Someone – "

But then it came again.

"G a i l . . . G a i l . . ."

"Someone calling my name."

Gail looked around but there was no one about. It had seemed to come from behind the wall.

"I can't hear anything."

"G a i l . . ."

It was a woman's voice, a little bit like her own, but sweet sounding, with an echoing quality, as if it was coming from the end of a tunnel. Nevertheless, it did seem to emanate from behind the wall. She walked up the drive to take a look. No one was there.

Over the next two weeks the same thing happened regularly, but as before, her mother heard nothing. To Gail it was as pure and clear as day. She told some friends at work and they just laughed. Her mother blamed it on lack of sleep, preferring that explanation to the more sinister one that Gail was 'hearing voices'. But she did not hear the voice at any other time, only at that spot. Because there was no rational explanation, she became afraid.

Gail was relieved when she was told that her job application to another company had been successful. She could start her new career as a cook straight away. This meant she no longer had to walk past the bungalow on her way to work.

The new job was a good excuse for celebration. Gail and a group of friends from the bakery decided to go out for a drink. Nothing special, a town centre pub then onto a club. It was a great night. Finally it was time for home. She ordered a taxi and it dropped her off on the new road near to the estate. Gail would take the short cut down the dirt track.

It was dark, and very quiet. As she neared the bungalow, Gail thought of the voice that had called out her name over the past few weeks. Was it trying to warn her of something? Just then she felt hot alcohol-fumed breath down the nape of her neck, and an arm closed like a clamp under her chin. The man breathed heavily as he dragged the struggling teenager past the wall at the front of the bungalow and onto the drive, where he fell on top of her.

Gail had no doubts what his intentions were. She managed to let out a scream before a spade sized hand slapped shut across her mouth. She had to do something quick. One hand was free, and she tried to prise his fingers away from her mouth. This was a mistake. He went for her throat instead and began to squeeze. Gail's hand circled about for something which might help her escape. She realised he meant to kill her first.

Suddenly a miracle happened. She felt a brick in her hand as if someone had placed it there. She brought it down hard on the back of the man's head and he collapsed on top of her. She struggled and pushed him off. The man was about six-feet tall and sixteen stones. He sat upright, his head in his hands. Just then a neighbour appeared awakened by her screams, but her attacker was already climbing to his feet and staggering off into the darkness.

Gail was in shock and could not talk properly for three months. There was bruising around her neck, but she could have been killed. Was the voice a manifestation of her 'guardian angel' warning her of the attack? Did this explain how the brick found its way into her hand?

The Cuerdly dragon slaying

Between Warrington and Widnes on the A562 is an area known as Cuerdly. Situated next to the mud flats of the Mersey is the site of Fiddlers Ferry Power Station. In the late 1980s one of its massive cooling towers collapsed during a violent storm. Just north of that is Bold which, until a few years ago, also boasted a power station. Both locations are on a line with one another. Most people will be unaware that Cuerdly and

Bold are directly linked with the slaying of a dragon during the Dark Ages.

Before man over-populated the area Runcorn was covered in a vast blanket of trees. Things lived in the forest, but supreme of them all was a fifty-foot long dragon which had its lair by the banks of the river. The beast terrorised the neighbourhood, carrying off sheep and cattle at its pleasure. Those brave enough to challenge it died alongside their livestock.

One of those least effected was Robert Byrch, a blacksmith who lived on Cuerdly Marsh. Robert had a fine reputation for the quality of his metalwork and was sought out by farmers and knights from miles around. He had seen the dragon and knew of the reward for its death, but none of his animals had been attacked so he was not unduly concerned. The reason for this immunity, he conjectured, was due to his animals congregating near the forge. The dragon, he reasoned, was probably afraid of the forge fire.

If so, was it hunger that drove the monster to overcome its natural fear? One day in November, while Robert was beating life into a ploughshare, the beast swooped out of the sky and carried off a cow from right outside the forge door. This enraged the blacksmith. It was one thing for his neighbours to lose their livestock, but another matter completely when one of his own animals was taken. Robert Byrch was determined to get his revenge.

His plan involved all of his professional skill and creative energies. Robert built a toughened and specially-jointed suit of armour which allowed him to walk on all fours. This was disguised with the skin and head of a cow. A shortened double edged sword was forged and attached to the armour within easy reach. Robert knew there were only two places on the beast where the blade could penetrate.

The dragon's scaly body was decorated with dark coloured broad bands. It flew by means of enormous wings, and its powerful jaws were armed with rows of saw-like teeth. Its heavily armoured body was vulnerable only under each wing.

It was a cold frosty morning just before Christmas when one of the blacksmith's apprentices spotted the monster circling in the sky. Robert donned his armoured suit, put on the disguise and walked out on all fours. With its glaring multi-faceted eyes the dragon spotted the 'cow', swooped down and carried it off.

The blacksmith drew his sword and stabbed it into the beast just beneath the nearest wing. Blood began to gush from the tear, and Robert sensed the creature weakening. At that moment he realised his mistake. The dragon was over the River Mersey. If it came down in the water, trapped in the heavy suit, he would sink like a stone and surely drown. Robert stemmed the flow of blood as best he could which enabled the dragon to limp back to its lair. Once landed it was too weak to turn on the man. He climbed out of the suit and finished off the huge monster, turning the muddy banks of the Mersey scarlet.

The heroic deed reached the ears of the king. He deemed that from that day, Robert Byrch should be known as 'Robert the Bold' and later was knighted. Further to this, the king decreed that Sir Robert should have as much land as the dragon skin could enclose. The former blacksmith cut up the hide into very thin strips and encircled the land around Cuerdly to be his. Robert was the founder of the Bold family and its huge fortune. But what are the facts behind the story?

Fiddlers Ferry Power Station at Cuerdley. Several UFOs have been sighted over its cooling towers and this was also where legend claims that a dragon was killed by a Saxon blacksmith. (Peter Hough)

The Bolds were probably one of the oldest families in the country. Their line stretches back before the Norman Conquest, and they may be of Saxon descent. The male line ended in 1762 when Peter, son of Sir Richard Bold, passed away. But was there a dragon slaying on the banks of the Mersey centuries ago?

The Griffin Inn on Warrington Road on Bold Heath once boasted a wall painting which depicted the aerial battle between the dragon and Robert Byrch. It was situated over the kitchen fireplace but was destroyed when some re-plastering work was carried out. Even more interesting is the skin which hung over the Bold family pew in Farnworth near Widnes. In 1870, after many centuries, it fell to the floor. This presented an opportunity for the dusty relic to be examined. It was pronounced to be the untanned hide of a cow – bearing strange claw marks.

5

MYSTERIES OF THE EAST LANCS ROAD

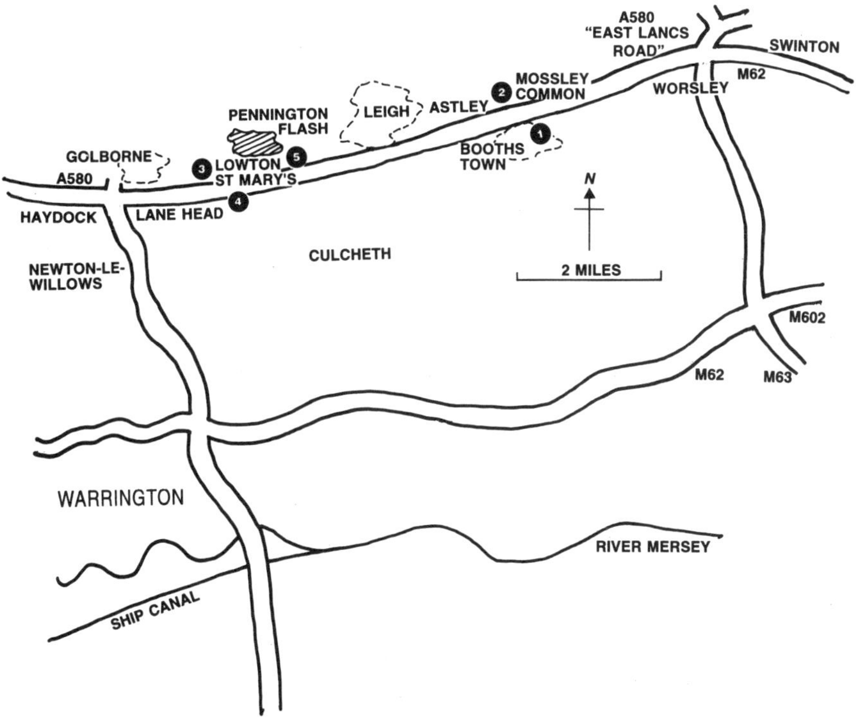

1.	Boothstown Abduction	2.	Mossley Common UFO
3.	Lane Head Phantom Jaywalker	4.	Lowton St. Mary's Ghost
5.	Greyhound/Leigh Alien Contact		

The northern boundary of the Mersey Valley

There are many mysteries associated with the A580, known locally as the East Lancashire Road. The dual carriageway was the successor to an older two-lane road. It links Manchester to Liverpool, and acts as our northern boundary for the Mersey Valley area.

There is a theory that roads constructed in the wrong places can disrupt natural lines of energy thought to criss-cross the planet. As we saw on page 58, where a disruption occurs, phenomena from other dimensions can manifest in ours. Accident 'black spots' are supposedly the result of this disruption. Can the theory account for Linda Tailor's experience?

Lights over the Lancs

Linda was in her late twenties in January 1981 when she was travelling home to Chorlton from Southport with her mother. At 7.30pm they saw a huge light in the south which seemed to be following their car. At this point, the vehicle started to jerk about and slow down. They were now at a point near Boothstown when suddenly an old fashioned looking car appeared before them, otherwise, strangely, the road was deserted. This distracted them from the light, but in the confusion the car disappeared!

They pulled into a service station and Linda went up to a man and pointed out a bright light in the sky resembling a metal disc. Suddenly it tilted and shot off. The two women continued home, where they discovered it was 9.30pm – one and a half hours later than it should have been! Linda felt nauseous and wondered what had happened to them. She was subsequently hypnotised in an attempt to explore the 'missing' time. Under hypnosis she described being in a strange white room.

There was some speculation by one investigator that Linda and her mother had initially seem the flare burning at the Carrington Oil Refinery. This would have been in the direction of the bright light, but Linda was unconvinced. Strangely, another UFO encounter was reported at the same place seven years previously.

On 14 October 1974 Mr and Mrs Haughton, an elderly couple who lived in Mossley Common, were witnesses to an unidentified aerial object.

Mr Haughton was disturbed at 1am by brilliant white light flooding into the bedroom. He awoke his wife, and thinking there was an accident, they climbed out of bed and went to look through the bedroom window. The window looks out in the direction of the East Lancs which is obscured by trees and buildings, about one hundred yards away. The light was not from emergency vehicles attending a road accident, it belonged to a huge object hovering just behind the trees. They gave a full description to Peter Hough.

The object had a domed top and a rectangular underside with seven framed 'windows'. White light was pouring from these square vents. As they watched, the thing rose to just above tree height and paused there for five minutes making no sound at all. The Haughtons were awestruck, but they retained enough composure to make some observations as to its size. Afterwards, they compared it to the length of a nearby barn, which turned out to be forty-feet long.

Without changing height, the object then began to slowly move away south, over Chat Moss. Suddenly, it dimmed perceptibly as it accelerated and disappeared.

Leigh ghost writer, Cyril Ward, reported on several tales of ghostly figures appearing on the East Lancs Road, before mysteriously disappearing. Indeed, Peter Hough interviewed a motorist who had such an experience on 8th October 1978.

Stanley Tranter was driving home with his wife after dropping her parents off. The car was travelling between the Greyhound Hotel near Leigh, and Lane Head junction at about 11.30pm when the incident occurred. Unfortunately, Mrs Tranter was asleep at the time. Suddenly, the car headlights picked out a strange figure walking towards them on the central reservation of the dark road. It was over six feet tall and wore a three quarter length coat with no apparent openings. Mr Tranter thought the garment was made of a highly reflective material because the figure was surrounded by an orange glow. However, when the car had passed by, Mr Tranter looked in his mirror and was amazed to see the figure still glowing brightly, even though the road was deserted.

Cyril Ward pointed out that the road split up many farms, and theorised that this 'must have confused many resident boggarts, spirits, hobgoblins and gremlins'. One elderly gentleman who lives at Higher Green, Astley, claims to have seen figures suddenly appear and disappear at the farm near the top of the lane where it meets the East Lancs

Road. Mr Ward speculated that a ghostly figure regularly seen crossing the road from Hope Carr towards Glazebury, might be the spirit of a Cromwellian soldier. Evidence of a battle has been found nearby.

The ghost of Cheetham Fold Farm

Between May 1884 and November 1885 the *Leigh Journal* published several articles relating to The Lowton Common Ghost. The A580 forms the boundary with the old common at Lowton St Mary's. Like most hauntings it was connected with a murder.

Joshua Rigby, known as 'Josh', was murdered at Cheetham Fold Farm by person or persons unknown. He was discovered with his throat cut. Josh was not well liked, and a local man was eventually arrested. The trial took place in the Jolly Carter public house, situated on Newton Road, just around the corner from the farm. However, the man was acquitted due to lack of evidence.

Josh was buried in St Oswald's Churchyard at nearby Winwick during September 1883. After the murder many local people, and

Cheetham Fold Farm, where Joshua Rigby was murdered in 1883 (Peter Hough)

outsiders too, believed they had encountered the farmer's ghost. In May 1884 a collier called John Smith was walking from St Helens to Bolton and passing through Lowton along Newton Road by Cheetham Fold Farm when something terrified him. He saw a man dressed in dark clothes cross right in front of him without speaking or making any sound at all.

Smith was so shook up by the experience he reported it to the police, and a P. C. Langhorn verified that the collier was perspiring heavily and seemed sincere in his fright.

Two months later the *Journal* reported that Josh's ghost was seen at noon during Thursday. The witnesses were haymakers who ran off after seeing a figure dressed in white of pallid appearance. During July witnesses described a bright light which appeared almost every night and floated above the house and farm yard before vanishing. The phenomenon was observed between eleven and midnight – the time of the murder.

The newspaper articles were mostly in a style of disbelief. In the edition dated 23 May 1884 the writer said: 'Let the few unbelievers take with them some stout sticks and use them freely on "Josh's" impersonator, and his ghost will be forever laid.' The *Journal* was very pleased therefore to publish a story in the 20 November 1885 edition which, it was claimed, went some way to explaining the mystery.

It was reported that two young men were secretly courting some servant girls who worked at a large house in Lowton. They carried out their clandestine meetings by approaching the back of the house across the common during darkness. On this occasion the men were tapping on a window of the house to attract the attention of the girls, when a figure dressed in a white sheet suddenly advanced towards them.

They ran in panic, but one of them tripped and fell. As the 'ghost' loomed over him, the man pleaded with the apparition to go after his friend instead. It was at this point that the 'ghost' revealed himself to be the younger brother of the prostrate youth, who had followed them and decided on a prank. No doubt taking the newspaper's advice, the other young man returned with several men armed with clubs.

Was that all there was to the mystery? Peter Hough interviewed the current owner of Cheetham Fold Farm and discovered that sightings of *something* had continued until very recently. Brian Johnson who took over the running of the farm from his father had several tales to tell.

"My father was ploughing once and saw this strange mist. I've seen it too. It changed shape as I watched and moved about the field. At one point it funnelled upwards, then collapsed again and became elongated. Although it was mist-like, it wasn't ordinary mist but something more substantial, nothing like I've seen before. I don't know what it was but it was not natural."

"People used to come from miles around to look for the ghost. Up until ten years ago they would turn up in their cars and go searching the fields at the back of the farm with flashlights. But since the area was landscaped, no one seems to have seen anything."

The man who cried 'wolf'

Often the acceptance of an unbelievable story depends on the credibility of the witness. What if a witness has a less than reliable past record – should we discount his story entirely? Or could it be like the parable of the boy who cried wolf? This involved a boy who alerted the villagers so often to a bogus wolf, that when the real beast appeared and began attacking sheep no one would believe him.

In the early hours of 9 May 1985, John Meredith* was riding his Suzuki motorcycle along the A580 on his way home to Rochdale. That much we know is true. A native of Liverpool, John and his fiancée, Mary, had left the claustrophobia of the city streets some months before for the rugged moorland around north Manchester. During this time John had regularly made the one hundred mile round trip back to the city to visit friends. That was why he was on the deserted dual carriageway this particular night.

He remembers stopping for petrol at an all-night service station at Haydock, where the M6 crosses the East Lancashire Road; then, a few miles further on, pulling over for a cigarette and a drink of tea from a flask. He left the headlamp on so he could see what he was doing. It was about 4.30am.

In the still early morning, he suddenly became aware of a humming sound from an adjacent field. Still clasping his cup, John walked through a gap in the wooden fence into the field. A silvery glow emanated from a dip in the ground some distance away. Before he could get any closer he became aware of two figures walking towards him. Instinctively he began walking back to his motorcycle when a voice said: "Don't be afraid". They were now just a few feet away, illuminated by the headlamp.

Although similar in appearance, they were of different sexes. The female was approximately five feet tall, her male companion just a few inches taller. Both had straight shoulder length blond hair parted in the middle, and were dressed in ski type suits made from a material resembling lurex. Each had an egg-shaped implement attached to a belt around the waist.

"Who are you, and where are you from?" John nervously blurted out. The woman, who did all the talking, replied: "We are from the third solar system."

Sensing the absurdity of the situation, John literally pinched himself. "But there's only one solar system", he said.

"In your galaxy", she ambiguously qualified.

"But what are you doing here?" he asked. The answer was: "We have to make some minor adjustments to our craft". At this point John became more relaxed and found himself asking all sorts of questions. How, for instance, did their 'craft' work? The female informed him the craft utilised the Earth's magnetic field and gravity as a source of propulsion, but declined a fuller explanation because it was beyond his ability to comprehend, she said. Then, as John remained beside his motorcycle, the odd couple walked back towards the glow in the field.

The humming suddenly became louder and the glow brightened. Then an object the size of two double decker buses, shaped like an elongated rugby ball, lifted from the hollow. It hovered for a few seconds, then noiselessly shot off at an incredible speed.

When he arrived home at 5am, tired and hungry, he decided to mention the incident to no one, including his fiancée. In his own mind he wondered if he had come across a covert military exercise, and two of the participants had been playing a game with him. He telephoned Manchester Airport but they could throw no light on it. As the weeks passed, he tried to forget about the strange affair. Then, on Saturday morning of the 13 July, John claims to have had some visitors.

Mary was out shopping at 11.15am when a knock came at the door. Two men stood in the doorway, one aged about thirty-six and the other about forty. Both were identically dressed in clothes which looked 'brand new'. They wore black business suits, white shirts, black ties and black shiny shoes. Clean shaven, their hair was cut in the 1950s style of 'short back and sides'.

In the road was parked a black Ford Granada estate, in show room condition. This was curious because it appeared to be an old model with big lights at the rear.

"Mr Meredith?" asked the older, taller of the two, in clear, correct English. "We believe you had a Close Encounter". John was amazed; he had told absolutely no one.

"How did you find out?" he asked. The man stared at him without replying. Something was very wrong. Their appearance and behaviour gave an air of unreality.

"Can we ask, Mr Meredith, do you intend contacting anyone about your experience?". John now became annoyed. Thinking they were government officials, he asked for some identification. Again there was no response, as if he had not spoken, and instead the man continued: "It is important, Mr Meredith, that this goes no further". Now John lost his temper. "Look here, it's my business, and I'll tell who I like, when I like. Now clear off!"

The two men turned away and John slammed the door. Then he decided to note down the registration number and complain to the police, but the car was already disappearing up the road.

Two days later John told Mary the complete story. She thought it was a joke and laughed, before realising he was deadly serious. She thought he should take the man's advice and tell no one, but John felt differently. As if to reinforce the original threat, two days later a car parked close to their home. It was dark blue and a man sat inside smoking a cigarette. He was there from just after tea time until they went to bed. This was repeated for four consecutive nights. On the last night John was so annoyed he went outside and made a great show of writing down the car's registration number. The car never returned, but the intimidation did.

It was a Friday night at about 11.30pm, about two months after the UFO incident. Mary had gone to bed early, leaving John downstairs watching television. There was a knock at the door. Cagily, he got up and answered it.

Standing there was a very smart man in his mid-thirties. He wore what appeared to be an RAF uniform. This comprised blue trousers and zip-up jacket with epaulettes sporting fancy white and blue stripes. On his peaked cap was displayed a pair of gold wings, with gold braiding around the edge of the peak.

"Mr Meredith?" the man queried. John nodded. "I'm terribly sorry to disturb you at this late hour, but I believe you've had a Close Encounter of the Third Kind, with aliens."

This terminology was devised by the late Dr Allen Hynek, and then used as the title for Stephen Spielberg's film. It was strange that both sets of visitors should use this term with a member of the public as if they were reading it straight out of a book.

"How have you found out about this?" John asked. The man smiled and shrugged his shoulders. "You know how it is, we have our sources." After the episode with the two men, this did not satisfy John.

"Before we go any further, I want to know who you are, and I want some identification. "

The officer produced a plastic wallet and flipped it open. Inside was his photograph, and inscribed beside it was 'Flt Lt Keen'. John felt more at ease. "How can I help then?" he asked. Keen looked decidedly embarrassed.

"This experience with the aliens. We just want to make sure you weren't thinking of publishing it anywhere – you know, newspapers, magazines, that sort of thing."

In spite of Keen's politeness, John told him he would not be dictated to.

"You've got to see our point of view," Keen replied, "it wouldn't look good for us with the public."

"Who's 'us'?" John queried. "You mean the military?"

Keen laughed. "You could say that!" Then he turned and walked away.

John Meredith subsequently contacted Peter Hough, and he and two other members of the Manchester UFO Research Association, Darren Egerton and Philip Whitehead, investigated the case. The story contained most of the elements of other stories, including the so-called 'Men in Black' – visitors who call and threaten witnesses after UFO events. However, to his credit, John was not including a UFO abduction in his account. There was no 'missing time', a feature of other, similar cases.

John was not sure exactly where he had stopped that night for refreshments, but the investigators pinned it down to a place between the Lane Head Junction at Lowton, and the Greyhound Hotel. 'Keen' remained an enigma, although an RAF Base Commander did confirm that John's description of the uniform was standard RAF issue.

On the minus side, John told Peter Hough that he had suffered poltergeist activity in his flat in Liverpool. He gave the author several names of people who, he said, would back up his claims. Peter contacted them but no one would corroborate the story. The Reverend Alan Jones who had been called out to exorcise the flat said he had seen nothing to convince him that anything anomalous was happening. It was speculated that severe mental stress Meredith suffered following his mother's death could be to blame.

Did the UFO encounter occur on the East Lancashire Road, as John Meredith patently believed it had? John is not an ideal witness, but enough detail emerged in his story, including the fact that his fiancée had also seen the man in the car, to make one wonder.

6

WONDERLAND

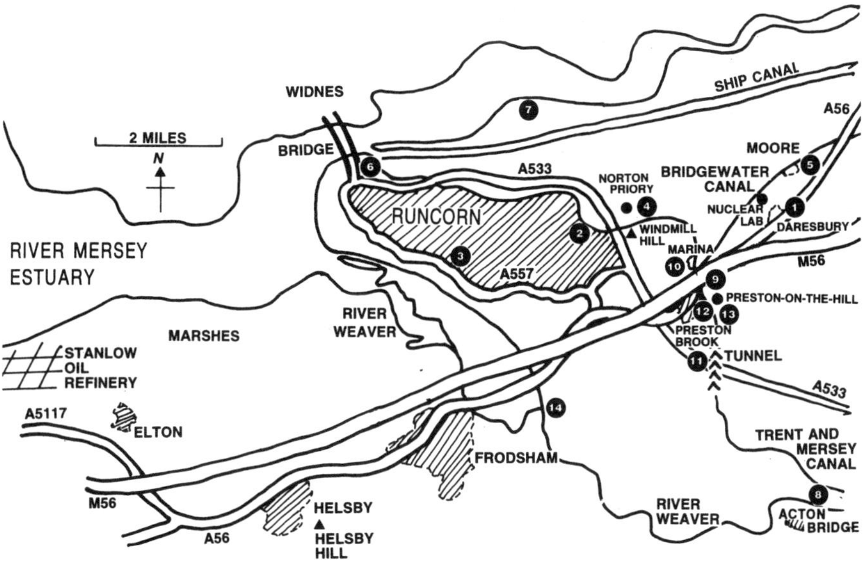

1.	Daresbury Car Teleport	2.	Runcorn Abduction
3.	Runcorn Poltergeist	4.	Norton Priory Phantom
5.	Moore Ghost Dog	6.	Runcorn/Widnes Bridge Ghost
7.	Mersey Estuary Ghost	8.	Acton Bridge Time Loss
9.	Preston Brook/M56 Abduction	10.	Preston Brook Marina Giant Bird
11.	Canal Boat Poltergeist	12.	Preston Brook Crop Circle
13.	Preston Brook UFO	14.	Frodsham Cownapping

The North Cheshire banks of the Mersey estuary

South of Warrington, north of Chester and east of Ellesmere Port lies a little triangle of land with magical powers.

In the heart of this region lies Delamere Forest, its tall pines thick on the sky line. This serves as an oasis of woodland in the deforested countryside. There is also north Cheshire's only hill of any real note, at Helsby, where the rocks are twisted into a simulacra of a human face which is visible as you pass along the M56 motorway from east to west.

The region is bordered to the north by the Mersey estuary, widening as it gapes open mouthed at the murky sight of the Irish Sea. This is lined with chemical factories and smoking chimneys as well as the glittering toy of the Runcorn-Widnes bridge, a last chance to hop across the river by conventional means. The occasional aircraft can also be seen in the sunshine, cruising low on the last lap into Speke like distant

Looking across the Mersey from Hale Head towards Runcorn – lair of a dragon in the Dark Ages and portal to a modern Wonderland. (Peter Hough)

herons sweeping along the river's surface on the prowl for something fishy.

Despite the intrusions of the present day, there is still a raw majesty about the deadpan, open vista that presents itself when you pass through Preston Brook and beneath the Liverpool to London railway track. This small, seemingly irrelevant dot upon the landscape acts like a key that unlocks a doorway into another world. For suddenly you can see the estuary spread out in tableau to the north and at long last sense the presence of the Mersey again after losing it amid the flat Cheshire topography.

But Preston Brook and Preston-on-the-Hill are doorways to more than just a spectacular view. They seem quite literally to show the way into a new reality. For here more strange phenomena per square mile have taken place than anywhere else surveyed by this book. This one small, rural area, is probably England's centre point of high weirdness; a supernaturally rare spot where anything can happen and usually does.

It earns the right to be called Wonderland which, as you will see, also turns out to be deliciously appropriate.

Alice's adventure in wonderland

The A56 plays a game of tag for quite a few miles in this region with the motorway that has stolen its number, the M56. They touch, then separate, then later touch again, as if engaged in some sort of ritual dance.

Just south of Warrington is Daresbury, with a large and pleasant hotel, a nuclear physics laboratory and, in truth, precious little else. But it also has another, less obvious, claim to fame. For here was born one of the world's best loved and most widely acclaimed fantasy writers, Charles Dodgson.

You will probably know him much better under his nom de plume, Lewis Carroll. For in that name he penned the timeless stories about Alice journeying into Wonderland to see the White Rabbit and the Cheshire Cat (now you know why it was not an Oxfordshire moggy that was immortalised). On another occasion Alice ventured into a mirror world beyond the looking glass and met all manner of bizarre creatures there.

It is an interesting metaphor to such stories that nuclear physicists are also probing through the looking glass into a magical world of sub-atomic particles which more than one scientist has ironically likened to Lewis Carroll's fantasy creations. They discover how particles appear like phantoms, do fantastic things and then pop right out of reality again. They sound exactly like the UFOs or ghosts we have been meeting! Certainly, they are every bit as cantankerous as the Mad Hatter.

Carroll would surely delight in the irony that his home village has continued an association with a secret doorway into hidden realities.

But it is deeper and becomes far stranger than that. For Daresbury sits at the gateway to a world of mystery that has unfolded here over the past century. It is almost as if Dodgson in the great beyond is somehow pulling the strings and revelling in the real life fantasies he can weave.

The essence of Wonderland is a small triangle of land with sides perhaps five miles long, roughly located between Helsby Hill, Runcorn and the villages of Daresbury and Moore. Unlike the mythical Bermuda Triangle, which is anything but triangular and covers an area of sea so vast that occasional strange things are simply bound to happen in it, Wonderland is different. Nobody can argue that this small, seemingly unimportant, mostly rural and hardly massive area of Cheshire country-side would be bound to attract the supernatural like a magnet. That is exactly what it does.

Locally there are some who think that passing on the road through Daresbury subjects you to interference from beyond. There are even tales that stage-coaches plying the route in the last century suffered. Horses would stop as if unwilling to travel further, then, just as suddenly move off again on their way to Chester.

Peter Taylor was not in a stage-coach, but the modern day equivalent, the horseless carriage, when he passed regularly through the village in winter 1973. He was then working as a building contractor on a pipeline nearby and for two successive nights found that as he drove past the Ring O'Bells inn the car engine failed. He got out but found nothing amiss with his two-month old vehicle, and it was later checked over and found perfect. He had to push it down the hill, hoping it might restart. After passing the hotel it had done so on both occasions and gave no more trouble.

A few days later he finished work at 7.30pm and was set to journey home when again he struck problems at Daresbury. This was becoming quite a curse by now, though he knew nothing about the traditions of the area. As Peter was still trying to fathom out why the engine was faltering everything was normal again, with one exception. He was lost. He found a call box to locate himself and stared at the dial. It advised that somehow, inexplicably, he was now in Preston, Lancashire, some 40 miles north. It was 9.30pm. Well over an hour of his life had simply disappeared from memory.

He called home and said; 'You are not going to believe this but . . . '.

After this Peter Taylor's car ran like a dream and he sailed through Daresbury without hassle. Yet others have not been so lucky.

One woman called us in summer 1988 to explain that her car had packed up on the road as she drove a few hundred yards from the physics laboratory. It just spluttered, died, the headlights went out and then came back on again. Nothing was wrong when it was examined. She had never heard of Peter Taylor nor his unpublished story but told us that she had enquired and other cars had similar problems on this road. "I think the physicists are up to some sort of experiment," she added, claiming that a friend who worked at the lab said they had received other similar reports from local drivers. We called them, but the lab scoffed, saying it was all just a story.

Maybe so, but this woman did have one unique qualification to make us take her seriously. Her Christian name, naturally enough, was Alice; curiouser and curiouser, as someone in a certain book once said.

Through the looking glass, via Zomdic

James Cook was always seeing strange lights over Runcorn. This is no big surprise. Some of them may have been aircraft heading into Speke. On the other hand, the odd goings on around the town do make it vulnerable to these sorts of peculiarities.

Anyhow, on 7 September 1957 Cook had received a message in his mind that 'they' were coming for him and so decided to forsake his bed and climb to a small Runcorn hill by a little reservoir and look out across the Mersey to await his destiny. At 2.15am, it duly arrived.

At first he just saw a light which changed colour as it drifted through the air. It blended from white to blue and finally to red, before descending only 20 feet away, now visible as a huge saucer almost 100 feet across. This did not land, merely hovered a couple of feet above the rain soaked grass, which was swaying in the breeze created.

As Cook stared in astonishment a voice entered his mind, telling him not to be afraid but to enter the craft. To do this he would have to jump onto a railed step that had emerged from the side of the object. Later he was told that 'they' could not land in wet weather because they used an electrical field and this would 'earth' itself through the moisture. If he had touched it and the ground simultaneously, he would have been electrocuted!

Evidently entranced James Cook did as directed and entered a room where he found himself surrounded by a glowing light pouring from an unseen source all around him. The voice told him to take off all his clothing, which he did without any quibble. He was then told to don a silvery one piece suit which had no seams or zippers. When, incomprehensibly, clad in this they told him to leave the craft and enter another that had landed beside them on the hill.

As Runcorn slept, James Cook says he was taken into space by this larger object. Here he met some very tall beings with human-like appearances but faces that were fresh and babyish. They claimed to be neither male nor female and to have no hostile intent towards the Earth. Rather, they were here to help us avoid grave dangers that we were confronting. To prove the point they decided to take him to their home planet, called Zomdic. It was so far away Earth scientists had never discovered its existence.

On Zomdic he was told a great deal about the visitors. They communicated by telepathy and hand gestures, indicating their intentions. They even tried to explain the propulsion system of their intergalactic machines; although all he understood was that the smaller saucer craft could not travel between the stars and were used only for 'short' hops from earth orbit to the surface. They generated an electromagnetic field in flight.

Cook was given an audience with a 'wise one' who said that he had to take a message back to Runcorn. This was short and sweet: "The inhabitants of your planet will upset the balance if they persist in using force instead of harmony. Warn them of the danger". Not unreasonably, Cook argued that he was an everyday sort of chap and the world was unlikely to listen to him. The alien leader replied with a sigh, "Nor anyone else either."

With this, James Cook was ferried home from this personal excursion into Wonderland and deposited back in Runcorn, which, nice as it is, was hardly the same as the exotic splendours of Zomdic. Forgetting the alien warning he touched the metal handrail as he leapt from the ship, burning his hand in the process as a tangible sign that he had not simply dreamt all this. He was surprised to discover that it was now almost 11pm on 8 September, some 45 hours after he had been taken on this trip of a lifetime.

James Cook was not Britain's first alien voyager. George King, a taxi driver from London, claimed that honour and was much in the news at the time Cook had his experience. King had founded the 'Aetherius Society' (named after an entity he communicated with). This had similar aims, to bring harmony to Earth. The Aetherians remain strong 40 years later and a key branch was set up in Warrington, where a church was established for a time in a garage.

Warrington and Runcorn merged as a combined 'new town' in the 1970s and they shared things on a spiritual level also. For, while James Cook never tried to emulate the success of the Aetherians, he did form a small local group of people to fulfil his promise to the wise one on Zomdic. This included psychic experiences and channelled messages, rather as George King also practised. Cook achieved some local notoriety as a result.

In November 1959 he claimed a second contact while on a hill at Frodsham, equally close to the heart of Wonderland. This time he went to Shebic. Planet Zomdic was never heard from again, though since James Cook's day, thousands have claimed to have met people from, or even gone with them to, other worlds. In many senses, Runcorn set a global precedent.

Hauntings in Halton

Runcorn has had many odd goings on across the years. Between August and October 1952 John Glynn's house in the town was the scene of horrific poltergeist activity. Furniture was thrown around with extraordinary violence by an unseen force. The police even set traps for the spook, maintaining a constant watch on the house. That did not stop the invisible hands from wrecking the bedroom, tearing bedding to shreds and throwing metal bedsteads against walls. Then, just as suddenly as it had started, it petered out; although stories imply that things have happened there since.

A phantom green light has also been reported in the sky for centuries, where, green being the colour of the devil, it was given such associations. This may be methane from the riverside marshes, of course.

Norton Priory, now largely in disrepair, sits behind Windmill Hill north of the Preston Brook interchange between the A56 and M56. It is midway between Runcorn and Daresbury and visible from the main west coast railway line from London to Scotland inbound to Warrington.

There are many stories about spectral music in the dead of night and apparitions of hooded monks that seem to date from centuries ago.

Just north of Daresbury is Moore. Here a retired nursing sister described the odd things that have happened in Wonderland. When working in a town hospital, she reported that a strange light was often seen by staff prior to a death on the ward. It became an accepted omen of doom.

Margaret Wilson* told of two particularly chilling experiences in Moore. She had returned home one day from visiting her husband in hospital, feeling very sad. She spread out the newspaper on the carpet to read it, as was a custom, when suddenly she heard a clicking noise. Instantly she knew this was 'Judy', her dog, which made the sound with her claws as they caught the nylon carpet.

Margaret was able to follow the sound right across the room until it simply disappeared. But Judy was not there. The dog was 'put to sleep' after an incurable illness had been diagnosed. This was some three months before.

In 1981 she had a dream in which her stepfather appeared. In reality he had died four years earlier but he seemed as large as life. In the dream, he asked Margaret to rummage through an old bureau, which she now possessed. As she touched the wood it decayed and out fell a pocket watch with both hands pointing to 12 o'clock. Two days later her mother passed away at exactly 12 midnight! The dream had seemingly foretold the decaying of the body and that her 'time was up', even predicting the exact hour.

But perhaps the scariest goings on come from a house literally astride the Mersey river bank, and only yards from the Runcorn-Widnes suspension bridge. Here the Jetsons had their excursion into Wonderland.

It began when Linda was alone with three-year old Lisa. Linda was watching TV but became aware of her daughter talking to somebody. Turning around she saw the girl crouched on the steps engaged in animated chat, apparently with thin air. She was having a one-way conversation with nobody.

Of course, children often invent invisible friends, but this was different. It took quite some effort to wrest Lisa from the stairs and, even when Linda Jetson did so, her daughter still kept glancing back from the security of the sofa and giggling. After half an hour she announced that her mystery friend had disappeared.

Three months later, it all happened again. Linda was reading a story to Lisa in the bedroom when she explained coolly, 'He's here'. Turning around and expecting to see Mr Jetson back home, Linda's heart thumped rapidly when it was clear that her daughter meant the invisible man again.

Lisa explained that he was an old man with white hair who was nice and friendly and wanted her to be good to her mummy. Lisa had promised this. "He calls me 'chuck'", the girl intoned, sending a chill through her mother.

Linda Jetson's grandfather had also called her this, something Lisa could not know. But there had been a family row and despite attempts at reconciliation, ties were cut. Lisa had not seen her great grandfather since just a few weeks of age. Only much later did the family learn that he had died a couple of days before Lisa first saw the odd man upon the stairs.

Next day Linda got out the family photo album and casually looked through it. Lisa was sitting nearby and watched idly, quite disinterested. But she then lit up when her eyes saw one man. It was her recently-deceased great grandfather. "That's him", she cried. "That's the man who comes to see me."

Highway robbery

Travellers on the roads to the south of Runcorn certainly have their problems. We have heard about the car stops around Daresbury and time also seems to be robbed from the lives of folk in this part of the world.

In 1977 we obtained a story from a security firm on the banks of the Mersey between Runcorn and Warrington. It was early morning and two staff were on duty, protecting a building site as part of the embryonic Warrington-Runcorn 'new town' housing development. They had to make calls every hour to report back to their main base in Warrington advising that all was well. Indeed, they had just made their 1.00am contact.

Then their little wooden hut was filled with blinding light as if a nuclear bomb had exploded outside. In terror the two men admit they hid under the table. Although the light was brilliant one man reported how it was oddly beautiful and hypnotic and he could stare without blinking.

For about 20 minutes the two men hid in the hut as a humming noise filled the yard outside. Then they were discovered by another security guard who had been sent out by base to find them. They were still under the table, although the object was not to be seen. He asked what they were doing and pointed out that headquarters had become very concerned because they had missed their 2.00am call. The guards thought that only 20 minutes had elapsed, but more than an hour and a half had mysteriously vanished.

One of the men was very experienced, the other a trainee, but both were absolutely petrified when found. They were so shaken that a company director had to be called from Warrington to pick them up and drive them both home. Upon inspecting the ground a white misty powder, like dry ice, was found at the spot where the guards say the object landed.

At a company meeting it was decided that the local paper should be notified and they could use the slogan, 'our security is out of this world', to excellent promotional effect, but the two men refused to have anything to do with publicity. They just wanted to forget the whole thing.

Billy Lowry had an equally unnerving experience when he was riding his motorcycle. Unwittingly he entered Wonderland and suffered the consequences.

Billy was returning north from Brighton heading towards Blackpool where he was staying with some friends. At 11.50pm on 1 September 1983 he had passed through Whitchurch, stopped to phone an estimated time of his arrival home and then set off on the quiet A49 en route to Warrington.

He recalls seeing a strange light in the sky ahead and stopping to admire it, but his next move was utterly crazy. Although he was now on a rural stretch of road, apparently between Weaverham and Acton Bridge, and there was, of course, very little traffic at this late hour, he decided to disembark from the machine, switch off the lights and stand in the middle of the road looking up at the sky.

Billy knows that he had placed himself in a very dangerous situation. He was on a bend in the road, lined either side by trees. Had a car come around at speed it would probably not have seen him and there could have been a terrible accident. Yet he felt compelled to act as he did.

Above him now was a dark wedge shaped mass with several lights on it. The object was drifting slowly and silently above him at a snail's pace. Billy stared up at it in awe and then the nightmare happened. A car did appear round the bend, its headlamps arcing upward and then towards him. But the driver had evidently seen the object too. The man wound down his window, slowed to a crawl and drove carefully around Billy, but he did not stop. Billy thought about taking a picture of the object with his loaded camera, but a voice in his mind told him not to do this.

The motorcyclist now knew that he had to get out of there, so he switched on his lights and rode off. There followed a moment of total confusion. Minutes before the incident, at what must have been around 12.30am, he had passed a sign indicating that Warrington was some eight miles ahead. Now he saw a sign telling him that he was four miles from Chester, a city not on his route. In fact, he was no longer on the A49 heading northwards but on the A56 from Preston Brook, through Frodsham and Helsby and heading in entirely the wrong direction (south west).

Baffled by this Billy stopped to reorientate himself. He also took out his travel alarm to check the time, and ring Blackpool to give a new estimate of arrival following this mystifying detour. But it was not 12.30am, as expected. The time was now 2.15am. Over an hour and a half had simply vanished, just as it had for the security guards on the nearby river side housing estate. Billy Lowry had also entered Wonderland.

Beam me up, Spotty!

We do not know what might have happened to the two security guards or to Billy Lowry during their 'missing time' in Wonderland. Would they have visited Zomdic or its modern day equivalent?

A case that might help us to answer this question also reportedly occurred in the same area and began in a similar way. But it had a curious, not to say disturbing, sequel.

In March 1988, both authors were working with Granada TV on the ITV charity telethon for that May, organising UFO-related events at the Jodrell Bank visitor centre at Goostrey in Cheshire. During our planning for this worthy event ITV advised us to contact a certain public relations firm who could help with our ideas. We did so and visited their Cheshire offices.

Here we learnt an astonishing tale about one of their employees who, apparently, was desperate to meet us. The young woman had only been with the company a couple of weeks, having moved recently to north Cheshire. She had suffered a terrifying experience on the night of 22 March.

At about 11.30pm she had been driving on the M56 from Liverpool and was just coming off the slip-road where the A56 leaves the motorway at Preston Brook and Daresbury, right in the heart of Wonderland. There was some indication of a light appearing ahead, then a mystifying black-out. The woman regained her senses quite bemused because the car was now further along the slip road and she was feeling numb and tired. Staring at the clock on the dashboard did not help much. This showed 6.00am and at first she assumed it to be wrong, but it was correct. Somehow over six hours of memory had vanished. Stranger still, the car and her legs were covered in dark blue spots. This looked like mud, as if she and the vehicle had been through a wet field.

Understandably concerned by all of this, the woman had wanted to meet us to talk over the matter. She had already seen her doctor to discuss the trauma induced by this nightmare and was looking forward to talking to two researchers whom she had been told knew about the subject. However, on the day we visited (a week after the incident) she did not turn up for work and had also been off without warning the day before. Her boss was said to be concerned for her welfare as she was not answering her phone at home. Had 'they' come back for her, it was speculated? We were asked to try to find out.

To be truthful, we were rather wary of the story. A public relations company conveniently discovering a case like this just as they are about to embark on some UFO gimmickry (albeit to raise money for charity) seemed rather a coincidence. However, what we knew and what neither this woman nor the company boss could possibly have known (because we had never promoted the fact and nobody else seemed to have yet discovered it) was that the incident could hardly have taken place at a more appropriate spot. That alone, plus the fact that we knew of at least two very obscure overseas cases that were almost identical, made us continue with the investigation.

We never adequately resolved this case. The tabloid press were informed (not by us) and alleged that the woman had been 'put to flight' by aliens which had 'beamed into the car alongside her'. Her concerned boss had called in extra-terrestrial sleuths to crack the mystery. Useful as this PR must have been for the agency and flattering as the portrayal of us might seem, it was largely untrue. We never had the slightest reason to think that the witness was on the run from aliens or had seen one in her car. Indeed, within 48 hours of being set the task and a week before any of this publicity, we had traced this woman's whereabouts and discovered that she was perfectly healthy and suffering no undue anxiety. She was no longer working for the company in question. None of the newspapers ever spoke directly with us, despite quoting us as if they had. Otherwise we could have told them this.

Of course, we had provided this information to her bosses and now advised the press of the facts. It made no difference. Their story depended upon the woman being missing. They even quoted a police inspector, although we had established with him that (just like us) he had checked the matter out when it was reported to him and had almost immediately found the woman. Police had consequently not been 'baffled' as quotes alleged.

All of this was very regrettable and you must interpret it as you feel appropriate. It seems that the woman had a genuinely odd experience in this mystifying place where strange things so frequently occur. What happened, if anything at all, in the missing hours may never be known as the media treatment of the witness ensured she preferred to forget all about it, and not explore it further as we might have liked.

In a very similar case in Hungary, three years later, a mud-splashed woman who awoke in the middle of a snow-covered field with no tyre tracks leading in or out later recalled a medical probe by strange little beings.

Getting the bird

The location where the office worker lost six hours is very mysterious, being at the motorway slip-road just yards from the Daresbury Hotel in Preston-on-the-Hill. If you move a few hundred yards south and west from here parallel with either side of the motorway you cross a farmer's field and reach the Bridgewater Canal at Preston Brook near a little marina used by boating holiday visitors. You can practically see the spot where the woman's car stopped. This square half mile seems to be among the most amazing in England, perhaps the world.

Reported to us is a case from Donald Smith who travels the canals of Britain on his boat. In September 1968 he and his friend were fishing for bream off the Mersey in the old marina at Preston Brook.

It was 11.30pm and dark, but they were using a flashlight to illuminate the waters. Two old barges were tied by mooring posts side by side in the water, 20 feet in front of them. These were heavy and at least seven feet wide. The men later tried to move them but found it impossible to even depress them into the water or to cause any ripples.

Yet, as they watched for fish to bite, a huge creature swooped down from the Mersey estuary right at them. It was the weirdest thing they had ever seen. The neck was yellow and the beak hooked. Yellow tufts hung over its three toes (two forward and one back) and the eyes were bright red and ugly-looking. Worst of all, the huge bird gave off a foul devilish odour.

But the most terrifying thing was its size. It was wider than the barges, with a wing span of at least 12 feet. It settled onto one boat and its enormous weight pushed the deck noticeably downward sending a wave across the water. It was, they said, like a truck with its rear doors open!

After regaining their composure Donald's friend cocked the trigger on his rifle, brought with him to shoot rabbits. At the click the giant bird literally vanished into nowhere, disappearing on the spot as if it had never been there. It clearly had been, however, because the barge now rose a few inches in the water and sent another huge wash across the surface to lap against the banks by the terrified men.

What this monster was nobody knows, but the two experienced hunters are adamant it was no ordinary creature. It was a fugitive from Wonderland.

Putting the wind up

Another fascinating case we stumbled upon involved intrepid TV weatherman Fred Talbot. Originally a school science teacher in Altrincham, Jenny had worked with him in 1982 on the children's TV series *The Final Frontier* and he had gone on to gain a professional career on the popular ITV magazine show *This Morning*, where his trademark was quickly established. He is seen standing on a huge floating map of England moored in the Mersey docks outside the studios at Liverpool.

Before then Fred had done many features with regional television, his chirpy personality winning him many admirers. The incident came in June 1988, only weeks after the office worker had had her strange teleportation along the M56 slip-road.

Fred was travelling by barge criss-crossing the waterways of North West England with reporter Steve Winstanley, filming as they went along for a nightly TV programme that recorded their journey and people they met. What they did not film (sadly) was an incident that occurred as they drifted under a long dark tunnel. Steve Winstanley told us what happened, which differed a little from the version first leaked by the Granada press office.

They were traversing an eerie part of the Trent and Mersey canal system, where it passes through a very long, narrow dark tunnel with a low roof. Passing under here is not for the faint hearted and boatmen have reputedly died in its claustrophobic spaces. Once you set off, daylight is quickly swallowed up.

This is what they were doing, bravely negotiating the passage, when suddenly, in the dim light, two cans lifted up out of a black plastic rubbish bag on the deck of the barge, sailed up into the air and fell into the water with an eerie plop. The press office said these were used baked bean cans, allowing a joke about wind to be made. In fact, we learnt, they were cans of beer. Possibly Granada TV thought it inappropriate to mention that fact lest it conjured up less than truthful images about the state of sobriety of the two men. Winstanley told us they were definitely 100 per cent sober at the time.

As to what had caused the incident, it seems that an unusual sort of suction or vacuum effect was thought most likely. Ever the scientist and rationalist, Fred Talbot was sure there was an explanation. It was like an invisible vortex picking up the cans, taking them skyward, then losing the energy and discarding them into the water. The effect was not dissimilar to the way in which hay was sucked up at Marple Bridge (see page 9) creating a crop circle. This, as you will see in the next few pages, may be more than a coincidental observation.

Steve Winstanley also told us something that the press office had not mentioned. Earlier in their slow drift through the tunnel system the two men had heard a very strange noise. It was like a terrifying animal, much louder and stranger than a rat. A sort of grumbling, growling noise. It echoed within the cavernous confines of the tunnel and the darkness, of course, made the experience even more frightening. Winstanley insisted that it was "much, much bigger" than a rat, whatever the creature was.

That two odd events like this should occur within this tunnel system is interesting enough. What is even more remarkable is where the tunnel is situated. If you leave the Marina at Preston Brook, where the monster bird appeared, and pass the field alongside where the car was stopped, you suddenly plunge into this world of darkness, under a railway and farmland. The tunnel system is a small variation on the twilight zone that we are calling Wonderland.

Circles of power

The farmland under which the tunnel passes is owned by Bill Whitlow at Preston-on-the-Hill. He advised us that there have been many stories of strange noises attributed by some bargees to the tunnel being 'haunted' by the spirits of people who have died while passing through. More specifically, there appear to be further strange suction and vortex effects.

We learnt this potentially invaluable information by accident when investigating yet another case which came to light in August 1990, happening right in the same spot and this time involving crop circles.

That summer there was intense activity and countless media stories about the circles mystery. Many crude hoaxes were perpetrated and got great publicity. But one case they all failed to record, despite it being the most obviously visible crop circle in north-west England, was the one that formed on the Whitlow's winter wheat crop. This sat alongside the

M56 and the canal. The spot where the car was transported along the slip road is so close to where the circle formed that it could barely have been any nearer, literally being located beyond the hedge in the same field!

The circle was not the first in the area. As far back as the 1940s, there have been reports of farmers finding them on land beside the Mersey at Elton and Frodsham Marshes, just four or five miles west. The 1990 version was bigger than those, some 60 feet in diameter and comprised a single area on the land that slopes down towards the canal at Preston Brook. The centre was complex, consisting of dozens of mini-swirls scattered about the crop.

We discovered that it was first seen in the field on 28 July 1990 and, at about 2am that morning, one of the villagers had heard a strange, screeching, wailing noise like a tornado. This woke her up and lasted just a few moments, but was not a police siren on the motorway. Similar noises have been heard in Runcorn before, often attributed years ago to 'demons' but implying some strange natural force must exist in this neighbourhood.

On 4 August, Jenny Randles was in the field inspecting the circle and taking photographs on request of the farmer before he harvested the crop to prevent possible sightseers vandalising his land. Jenny's parents parked their car off the A56 by the gate in a way that police were later said to be satisfied with. They sat talking and having a drink of tea as they waited for their daughter's survey to finish. However, it ended in disaster.

Mr Randles saw in his rear view mirror a car swerve across the road as it climbed from Preston Brook towards the motorway slip-road. Moments later it slammed into their specially fitted Motability vehicle adapted for Jenny Randles' parents, who are both disabled. The car was destroyed by the impact and Mrs Randles had to be cut free of the wreckage by a fire crew, although both she and her husband later recovered in hospital.

The driver of the other vehicle told police that as he approached the field he suddenly lost control and was pulled across the A56 straight at the gate leading into it. He had no way of regaining control before his car was pulled into the back of the Randles' stationary vehicle, the only obstacle along hundreds of yards of open road.

Police conducted a major investigation but could reach no conclusions and establish no obvious cause for the accident, which wrote off a nearly new £10,000 car and caused serious injury to two people. It was as if an unseen force had tugged the unfortunate man's vehicle across the road towards the field where the mystery circle lay.

That this accident occurred only yards from where the office worker's car was inexplicably 'moved' in March 1988 is certainly peculiar. That so many other strange events involving cars stopping and 'teleporting' have also been recorded here is equally weird. To this we must add the strange noises, the poltergeist effects and scary sounds in the tunnel passing beneath the fields, the crop circle and the monster bird which appeared beside the canal, and we begin to see why this area is so fascinating. Clearly it is at the heart of some bizarre energy focal point which is not easy to comprehend.

Indeed, events at Preston Brook continue to occur. On 20 May 1992 at 10pm Graham Clamp, his wife, two children and their neighbours all saw a pink ball appear in the sky from their home at Cottons Bridge, Preston-on-the-Hill. It was over the Mersey in the north west and remained there for some moments, before fading to a white colour and then moving in a strange zig-zag course silently across the sky towards

Preston Brook, August 1990, showing the crop circle and the view west towards the canal where the giant bird almost sank a barge. (Jenny Randles)

the south, crossing motorway, canal, Helsby Hill and then disappearing in the direction of Chester.

It seems that Wonderland remains as busy as ever.

Rustlers from outer space

What exactly is going on in Wonderland remains to be seen, but its status as a window area is surely undeniable. Pause on your way along the Mersey Valley to think about the strangeness that seems infused within this small, unobtrusive country area and ponder what it means.

That it has generated strange phenomena for a long time is suggested by the colloquialism given to the location of our final story. This is two miles to the south of Preston Brook, just outside Frodsham and beside the banks of the River Weaver, which here flows north and west into the Mersey estuary through a series of meanders, weirs and marshy flood-plains. The lush farmland at this spot is known as the Devil's Garden. In January 1978, the 'Devil' took the astonishing form of cattle rustlers from outer space.

Four youths, in their late teens, one the son of a local establishment figure, hence their desire for anonymity, were poaching for pheasant on the evening of 27 January – another reason for their desire to avoid publicity!

Suddenly they spotted a strange object floating along the surface of the Weaver from the south and east, thus being in the vicinity of Acton Bridge where Billy Lowry entered Wonderland five years later. As it came closer it resembled a dome, slightly truncated at the base but with a skirt like a hovercraft. It was well above the water's surface, perhaps at rooftop height, with what looked like firey 'retro rockets' on the under-side.

The men first thought they were observing a satellite. This odd conclusion was probably fuelled by a recent news story where a Soviet nuclear powered satellite had crashed in the wastes of Canada, provoking quite a fuss. However, their view that this object was another example was not to last long, because the thing left the river and came to rest in the field a hundred feet or so in front of them. As it did so it made a humming sound coupled with a rushing or screeching not unlike the wind at high speed.

The dome-like craft, some 15 feet in diameter, was now on the ground near to the men, shining silver in the dark night with a strange purple glow coming from a line of windows on its edge. This was fuzzy and hurt their eyes if stared at and seems to have been ultra-violet in nature.

Frightened now of radiation poisoning they decided to get out of there as fast as they could, but just as they were about to leave a figure emerged from the machine. This man looked normal, though slightly small in stature, and was encased in a one-piece silvery suit. The only notable feature was a helmet with a light on the top, rather like a miner, but this emitted the same fuzzy purple glow as the windows.

The figure looked around as the men crouched behind bushes and, thankfully, ignored them and focused on a small group of cows standing immobile close by. Returning to the object a second figure came out to join the first and both carried a large frame, like a clothes horse, but larger. It looked like it was made out of thin tubing, and the men assumed this was something very light, perhaps aluminium, because the two small beings had no trouble carrying it.

The entities took it to one of the cows and placed it around the body like a cage. The cow made no movement or sound. Nor did the others in the herd. The figures then moved the struts and bars around as if taking precise measurements of the poor beast.

The four men had by now had enough, concluding they might be next on the list after the cattle. They fled across the fields towards the bridge that carries the A56 over the river, a mile or so from the centre of Frodsham. They did not look back until they reached the safety of the road, but by then the object had vanished. They recall nothing further and were paying no real attention to the time so it is not absolutely clear whether there may have been any missing period.

However, as they ran away one of the men, who possessed science qualifications, told us of a sensation he had felt. He did so in what were clearly very embarrassed tones. He described a 'tugging' in his nether regions as if there was a suction device pulling at his testicles. For two or three days afterwards his legs were red and swore as if suffering from sunburn, which is, of course, quite impossible in Britain in mid winter.

Emmy award winning TV producer Linda Moulton Howe has researched other cases with links between human abduction and cattle rustled by alien beings. She produced a documentary and book called *An Alien Harvest*, assessing how a genetic experiment may be afoot to reproduce hybrid entities. The Devil's Garden case, reported before many more recent examples, especially in the USA, may be a significant early record – of something!

7

WEIRD WIRRAL

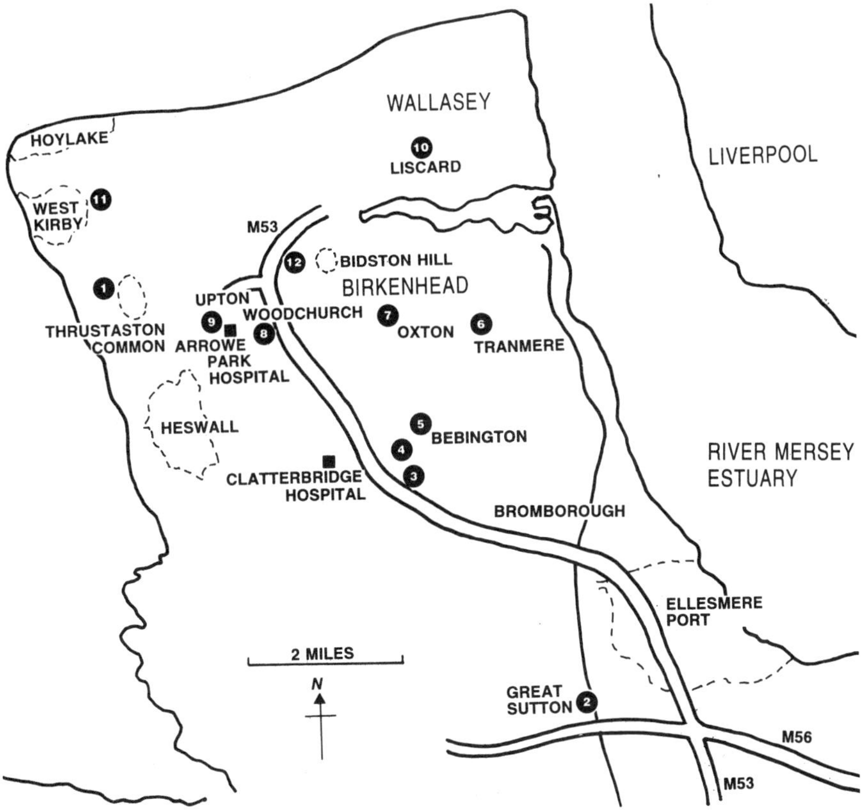

1.	Thurstaston UFO	2.	Great Sutton Triangle
3.	Clatterbridge Lights	4.	Clatterbridge Phantom Hitch Hiker
5.	Bebington Dancing Gnome	6.	Tranmere Poltergeist
7.	Oxton Ghost	8.	Arrowe Park Phantom Phone Call
9.	Arrowe Park Hospital Near	10.	Liscard Poltergeist Death Vision
11.	West Kirby Vision	12.	Bidston Hill Hauntings / UFOs

The Wirral Peninsula of North Cheshire and Merseyside

As the Mersey reaches its ultimate goal, the Irish Sea, there are two ways of watching its fulfilment and gazing upon the ocean-going ships. You can do so from the ancient but recently transmogrified docklands of Liverpool or the timeless countryside of the Wirral, one of the few true peninsulas in Britain.

There has always been a fierce rivalry between the two. Liverpool, a prosperous port famed the world over, was Lancashire's chief outlet for its trade and industry that enabled Britain to rule much of the globe during the industrial revolution. The Wirral, with its smattering of isolated villages and the fast expanding eastern towns of Birkenhead and Wallasey, was part of Cheshire and proud of the somewhat upper crust image that this suggested.

The creation of Merseyside, bridging the two sides of the Mersey estuary in a metaphorical bond, just as the centuries-old ferries and newer road tunnels had physically achieved, was viewed with much distrust 'over the water' (as locals call the divide into the Wirral). There are still many who refuse to accept they are no longer in Cheshire, wherever County Liverpudlians think they reside these days.

Wallasey is a town without a centre, formed from an aggregation of villages (such as Leasowe, Poulton and New Brighton). Once an island, it was walled off against the sea (hence the name). Shipbuilding in Birkenhead has breathed its last and the two differing towns have merged into a steady stream of housing to mirror the city a mile away across the river mouth.

New Brighton was named to emulate the south coast's posh seaside town; but it has lost its tourists, ferry boats, tower built to rival Blackpool's famous monument and, many fear, most of its charm. It is now barely distinguishable from any other part of the conurbation; but planners fight on with a bold bid to bring trams back to ply a new track!

The Wirral is largely flat, but with one fascinating hill. Its 15 mile length and 9 mile width is full of contrasts, from western marsh, to southern farm, and from eastern town to northern beach. It is certainly a unique part of north west England with strange phenomena to reflect that fact.

The South Wirral lights

Strange lights have often been seen over the southern part of the peninsula. At about 2.30am on 12 July 1981, the crew of a Dan-Air cargo plane, inbound to Liverpool across the Wirral, observed something odd. This was just after reporting in over the Point of Ayr lighthouse on their way from Belfast.

The light was described to us as like a huge white bulb, much brighter than another aircraft and closer to the ground. Although it was related immediately by radio to the air traffic control, who apparently had nothing else on radar at the time, and also to ground staff after touchdown, the crew chose not to make an official report. We were told that airlines often prefer not to make such matters public since it tends to be more trouble than it is worth.

Nevertheless, the same phenomenon was independently reported to us by Keith Daniel and a friend, who could have had no idea about the unpublicised Dan-Air encounter. They were on Thurstaston Common just north of Heswall, affording a splendid view westward. It was just after 2.00am on a night in July 1981. Investigation has since proved it to be the same date (ie the 12th). They were with a group of one-parent children on a camping trip and were relaxing after settling them down for the night. They saw the yellow/white light hovering low over a factory with a red aircraft hazard light on top. As they discussed what it was, suspecting a helicopter, it changed to a dazzling blue/white and shot across the sky out of sight as fast as a bullet. They told a park ranger next day, but got the impression these lights were so frequent that few were perturbed by them.

However, a more substantial incident occurred on the night of 18 May 1975. An object may have actually landed on the other side of the Mersey estuary.

The incident began there, at Rainhill, near where the famous railway trials launched the world's first passenger railway line. At about 10pm Mr and Mrs Scothern observed three bright lights in a triangle (very similar to those seen by the police officers at Cheadle Heath 13 years later, see page 16). However, these came down at a steep angle to apparently land inside a little clump of trees. The witnesses went to the site, noticing a glow coming out of a hollow. However, after fetching reinforcements and returning to the scene, nothing was visible in the darkness.

Next morning, in daylight, the area was carefully searched. A small duck pond with heavily caked mud was inside the hollow. Here a strange metal coil was discovered, and analysis revealed this to have been made from fairly pure aluminium. Nearby were four footprints, beginning and ending in the middle of nowhere despite the mud all around. These were very large, peculiar in the form of squares and deeply imprinted. The stride length between them was big, almost four feet.

Five years later we discovered another witness to the same incident, Daniel Cheveaux and his family at Great Sutton. They saw the same triangle of three lights, appearing in the south near Chester and heading off north westwards. It was on the same date in 1975 but at 10.50pm, some 50 minutes after the landing across the water.

Daniel was able to look at the lights very closely through binoculars but there was no structure behind them. He had become well used to seeing aircraft in the area, as these pass over on their way to Liverpool Airport all the time, but he insisted that this was something different.

We can be absolutely sure that the two events match because Daniel was so impressed by his own encounter that he scribbled a full account of it, with date and time, onto the side of a cupboard door in his house. So even years later it was there to remind him of the facts; although what his mother had to say on this unusual way of keeping notes is not clear!

More recently some very similar lights were seen passing over Hooton and investigation there suggested that a Britton-Norman Trislander aircraft might possess the same lighting configuration. One of these had been heading down the Mersey at the time on a trip from the Isle of Man.

However, this seems unlikely to have been responsible for the case in 1975 when these aircraft did not fly into the airport. The triangle of three lights is a remarkably common type of phenomenon, seen under other circumstances when there is no possibility that it was an aircraft.

Investigators refer to this mystery phenomenon as the pawnbroker's sign, because of the resemblance to that symbol. However, some sceptics have suggested other acronyms which they regard as rather more appropriate for a load of lights in the shape of balls.

Clatterbridge curiosities

The M53 motorway leaves the M56 just south of Ellesmere Port and runs right up the spine of the Wirral. You can pick it up at Hooton, scene of the above incident and three or four miles further north you will skirt Bromborough and reach Clatterbridge, where there is a famous hospital. This stretch of road has some very interesting stories connected with it.

Another witness to the south Wirral light spotted it here while driving in his car. He was on the M53 with his daughter and two friends around dusk, one night in September 1980. As an amateur astronomer he was puzzled because he could not identify the source of the brilliant glow in the south-east. So he drove off the motorway and stopped at a convenient spot near the hospital, watching now as the light zig-zagged across the sky in a wide triangle. There was no sound as it flew and when it disappeared, it 'definitely moved and did not just go out'. It shot to the horizon at incredible speed, exactly like the light seen from Thurstaston had done.

Jenny Randles suggested to the witness the possibility of what is termed an 'earthlight', energy triggered by forces in the earth's rocks, riding on a magnetic cushion. He seemed relieved by the idea indicating, with a wry smile, that he had been worried they were about to come back for him.

This sighting is akin to so many others in the area, but has a special significance because of the name of the man driving the car. He was Gerry Marsden, lead singer from the famous musical group, Gerry and the Pacemakers, whose hits include the renowned Liverpool FC anthem 'You'll never walk alone' and 'Ferry Across the Mersey'.

This stretch of road also has a phantom hitch-hiker. In early 1970, a woman walking home from Clatterbridge Hospital saw a girl standing on the roadside as if waiting for a lift. As she approached her, the figure melted away into nowhere. She had vanished in just an instant. In July that year the figure was seen again by a motorist nearby, but the most chilling experience befell a man driving on Poulton Road in Higher Bebbington, just off junction 4 of the M53. A woman with a long dark coat appeared by the roadside and he slowed to a halt to give her a lift. But, as he opened the door to let her inside, she simply disappeared in the blink of an eye. Legend has it that she may be the spirit of a young girl who had left Poulton Hall on her way to a nunnery. Is she still trying to complete her last fatal journey?

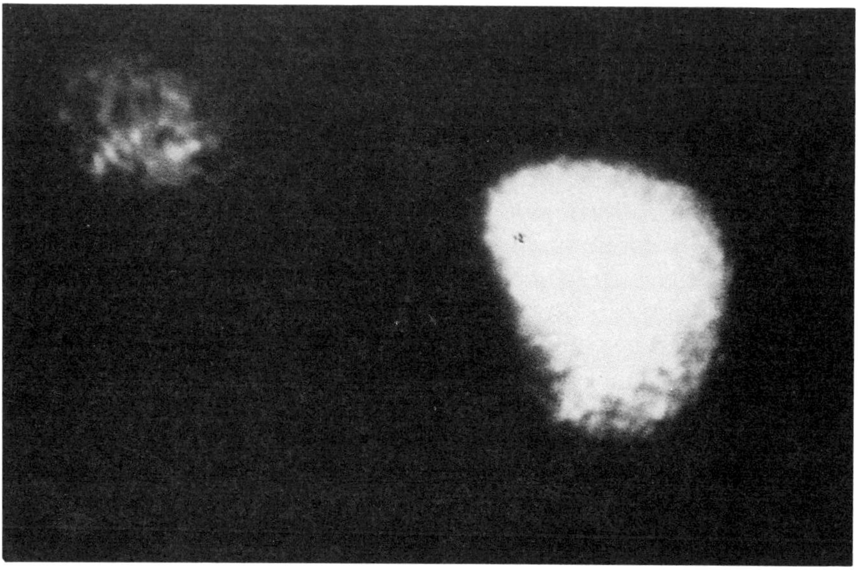

An 'earthlight' – the strange mass of energy formed, it is thought, by the physical pressures on quartz rocks (similar to piezoelectricity) causing energy to be squeezed into the atmosphere. These lights were filmed over a remote valley in Norway where they commonly occur. (Project Hessdalen)

The curse of the garden gnomes

Although this might sound like the script for a send-up of an Indiana Jones movie, we are assured that it is meant to be a very serious account of real events.

It came about when Grace McDonald*, a retired senior nurse in Bebbington, contacted us about the white footballs of light that kept appearing outside her bedroom late at night. They would hover there, drift over rooftops and then shoot away at great speed.

Grace suggested that most people do not see them because they do not look at the sky often enough, although there is no shortage of Wirral residents who do.

We then discovered that Grace was plagued by a terrible noise in the middle of the night, which at times when the lights are also there can sound like 'a thousand marbles rolling down the roof'. On other occasions it is more subdued and may be the hummadruzz that we first met in Manchester (see page 28). It seems to us that the hum, strange lights and other phenomena often go hand in hand.

When Grace first heard the hum as a child she was awoken by it to find a patch of light, like a torch beam, projected onto her bedroom wall. It was bright like the moon. As she stared at this a small figure, like a gnome, complete with a pointed head (or cap), appeared within the glow and smiled at her. He then started to dance and spin around, staying in the circle of light, which remained static.

After watching this for some moments, mesmerised by the experience, Grace let out a scream. This brought her father scuttling up the stairs and switching on the light. Just before he arrived the gnome and the circle of light disappeared. However, it left Grace with a legacy.

For a start she knew that she was going to see the figure again at some point in the future and that when she did it would not be in a circle of light but at much closer hand. She was not especially scared by that fact but it had an ominous foreboding to it.

As time went by, Grace had several strange experiences and also began to develop what was virtually a phobia about gnomes as a source of fun or amusement.

This began when her mother purchased two of them as ornaments and somehow Graçe knew that this was not going to be appreciated. She felt that it might anger someone, or something. So she begged her mother to dispense with them. She refused and shortly afterwards died under tragic circumstances.

From that day onward Grace went on a sort of crusade to try to prevent the people of Bebbington from owning garden gnomes. She had some success stories but failures too. One woman who refused to bin the offending creatures lost both legs in a serious accident. Another woman's husband was rushed to hospital and, seeing this as fulfilment of Grace's prophecy of doom, immediately got rid of her garden gnomes.

Grace McDonald told us that she felt the gnomes have to be given respect and the disasters stem from people treating the ornaments frivolously. We are certain that she is utterly sincere in this quest.

There was an oddly similar episode involving two men skiing through snow-bound woods at Imjarvi in Finland in 1971. They also spotted a strange little creature with a pointed head that was standing in a buzzing circle of light, projecting a beam from a box. They suffered major physical illness as a result, which according to doctors was similar to radiation sickness.

The images that the men at Imjarvi drew are not only reminiscent of those Grace McDonald told us about, but, according to researcher David Barclay in his book *Fatima: a close encounter of the worst kind* were also very similar to the entity seen in that Portuguese village in 1917. Witnesses here believed that the tiny figure was the virgin. A religious miracle is believed by many Catholics to have occurred at Fatima and was associated with major prophecies of global disaster, including (Barclay says) the catastrophic and still mysterious 'flu epidemic' of 1918 that killed 20 million people, World War Two and a third prophecy that a stunned papacy had long promised to reveal, but when the time came backed out of in 1960.

If you feel like smiling at Grace McDonald's story ponder how peculiar it is that these three quite independent and very different episodes in three countries all involve balls of light, buzzing noises, visions of gnome-like figures and disastrous consequences directly associated with each.

A Tranmere rover

Kevin Downes* is quite a rover, having moved around Britain. But he has never forgotten the incidents that occurred during his childhood in a haunted house near Prenton Park in Tranmere, Birkenhead.

They began about 1955 and involved the usual plethora of poltergeist effects. These included room lights switching on and off by themselves and peculiar crying or sobbing noises that began in the middle of the night.

On one occasion, Mr Downes father had a nightmare experience. He got up at 3.30am to visit the toilet and he suddenly began to lose consciousness. Mrs Downes found him being flung against a wall by an unseen force and fighting against someone, or something, that was trying to grab hold of him. Later he recalled a vision in his mind of a monk holding a book upon which 'a figure eight on its side' was inlaid. When shown the mathematical symbol for infinity he recognised this as the image on the book.

Kevin himself had a particularly odd experience one day in November 1967. He was walking by the park to a friend's house, a journey of only moments, and found that there was a thick winter fog. But, then he was struck down by a terrible force from above. It was an incredible rushing noise and sensation that seemed to be falling out of the sky.

Not surprisingly, Kevin immediately dived for cover onto the pavement and covered his ears because the sound was deafening. However, this act failed to stop the phantom noise. Then, in an instant, it simply disappeared.

He ran to his friend's house and rushed inside to ask what was going on; his friend was mystified. He had heard no noise. Kevin could hardly believe this. The incident had happened only yards away and it was so loud that half the town should have been in the streets trying to find out what it was. Of course, the fog might be preventing them from doing this, knowing that it was too dense to see anything not directly in front.

Fog? What fog? His friend was even more bemused now, leading Kevin to the door to reveal a crisp, sunny day. There was not a hint of the pea souper that only moments before had engulfed the teenager. According to his friend it had been clear all day.

The Brookside spectre

Under a mile from Kevin's haunted habitat is an old, imposing Victorian building, just off junction 3 of the M53 at Oxton, Birkenhead. It was built in the 1890s by a wealthy cotton broker family but the three floors have since been converted into separate and very spacious flats.

In 1978 actress Doreen Sloane moved into the top flat with her family. Doreen, who tragically died not long after we interviewed her, was a warm and friendly person, loved by millions because of her role as Annabelle Collins in the hit TV soap opera *Brookside.* She told us of the phantom with whom she and her family shared their lives, with typical compassion.

About six months after they moved into the flat Doreen began to feel a presence, though not an unfriendly one. Once, when alone in the house, she saw a shadow going into one of the bedrooms and assumed it was one of her two daughters who were both living there at the time. However, she checked and the house was completely empty.

The shadowy figure was seen on more occasions, and as time went by a little more clearly. It glided down the hall and into rooms making no sound whatsoever. They did assess all sorts of rational solutions but none made sense. As Doreen pointed out, being so high up, "It would have had to have been a very tall window cleaner."

Peter Hough pictured with the late Doreen Sloane. (Peter Hough)

Other experiences continued, one of the oddest being the smell of cooking that would appear in the rooms; it was clearly inside their flat and not coming from the outside.

Although the history of the house was not fully known to her, Doreen admitted that she kept getting a feeling that a large family had lived there who had been very happy, and that what was now their flat had once been the children's nursery. They had been fed here by a governess and this might be where the food odours originated from.

That this was not imagination was proven by the fact that other family members experienced all the same things too, although Doreen said nothing to them before hand. Her eldest daughter was with her one day when the figure went by. Doreen said, just in passing, "Oh! That must be the ghost" and her surprised daughter, noted: "So you've seen it too."

Sarah, then a radio presenter with Marcher Sound in North Wales, had seen the apparition on quite a few occasions, it turned out.

Doreen offered the most persuasive thing that had happened. One day she was in a walk-in cupboard in the room. The door was wide open. Sarah was in the room, but in the far side by the window. Suddenly Doreen turned around and the door was shut, trapping her in the darkness. She tried the handle desperately but it would not budge.

Calling out to Sarah she asked her to stop joking and "pretending to be the ghost". Sarah, protesting her innocence, spoke from what was clearly well away from the door, explaining where she was in the room and how she could not have touched the cupboard. Suddenly the door just burst open.

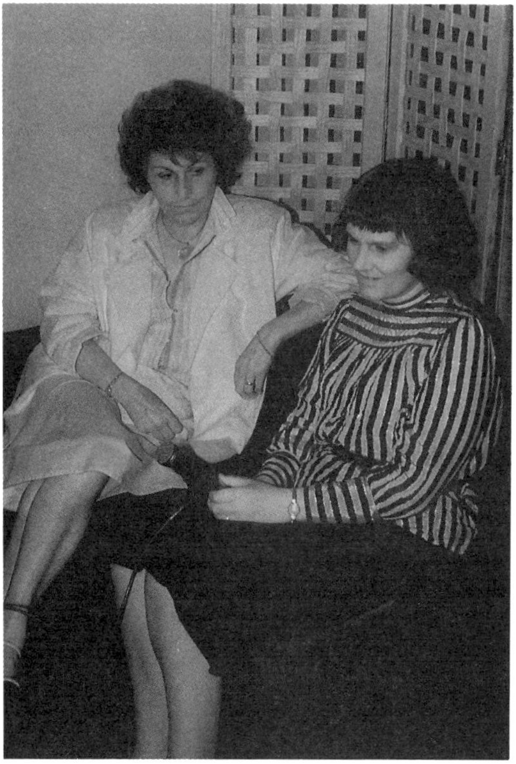

Jenny Randles interviews Doreen Sloane on the set of 'Brookside'. (Peter Hough)

Apparently this sort of thing happened often, with doors either opening or closing all by themselves, sometimes both of them in quick succession when nobody went near them and when every precaution had been taken to ensure that the cause was neither draughts nor the family cat, Emma.

Emma herself was not immune to sensing the presence. For four consecutive days, at the same time every evening the cat's fur raised up and she stared at something that she, but not the family, could see. She would run down the hall, try to escape, but fail, then cower under the table. She was clearly terrified by something.

By the fifth night, Doreen Sloane had had enough of this. So she spoke into the empty air, mindful of how silly it sounds in retrospect. "Please, ghost, you are frightening my cat. You can see how she reacts. She's terrified of you. Please don't do it", she requested pointedly. From that day onward, Emma was never frightened again.

Doreen was never herself frightened. She was convinced that the family that once lived happily in the house were pleased that another large and loving family were now in occupancy and were welcoming them.

Indeed, the thought never entered her head of trying to exorcise this particular phantom. After all, Doreen had pointed out, "I am just delighted that it is pleased we are here. I think it came back to check that everything is all right. But it is the ghost's house. The ghost was there first."

Heaven must wait

Lucia Randles is a fascinating woman. Completely unrelated to the co-author of this book, they met at Arrowe Park Hospital, mid-way between Oxton and Thurstaston in August 1984. They shared a remarkable experience just as they shared a small four-bed ward there.

Lucia had led an amazing and long life. Raised in Dresden, Germany, her father had saved his family from certain death in February 1945 by having a premonition of disaster and steering them to safety. This came on the night of the infamous allied raid that flattened this proud and cultured city which the locals thought immune because of its art treasures. Yet the bombing wrought upon it was more horrific and deadly than that of Hiroshima, and some consider it one of the most needless acts of World War Two, then only two months from its end in Europe.

After surviving the nightmare firestorm that raised the city to the ground, facing wild animals escaped from the zoo, Lucia was then forced to flee her family forever. She ran through land infested with victorious Russian soldiers on a wild rampage that became a frenzied orgy. She reached the west, met and married a British soldier, and returned to Birkenhead with him.

However, in July 1949 Lucia had an astonishing phone call from her spouse while doing the ironing during a fierce electrical storm. She picked up the phone without thinking, heard him say that he loved her but was 'so far away' and then realised that her hand was clutching empty air. They had no telephone! Shortly afterwards Lucia discovered that her husband had somehow forged a psychic link with her as he lay a mile away dying. He surprised a car thief outside his town centre office and was fatally shot.

Three weeks later, during another night filled with static, Lucia heard a buzzing or crackling and had the urge to pick up the telephone again. This time she remembered they did not have one. There was a burst of light at the window and a tiny ball of light appeared inside her room.

The light was about tennis-ball sized and was moving around, fizzing as it did so. She had very fine, long hair and this was attracted towards it because of the intense static electrical charge. Then suddenly it just disappeared. Lucia regarded this as a sign from her husband that all was well and she regained her strength of will which had been fast ebbing away.

Although we can make no presumptions about her interpretation of this event nor explain away the phantom phone call, we can know what it was that floated around her room. This was a rare atmospheric phenomenon known as ball lightning.

This is now accepted scientifically as a physical phenomenon. It usually appears as small balls that float freely, both indoors and outdoors, and while it often appears during thunderstorms does not seem to need them to do so. Powerful electricity in the air would be the trigger required. Ball lightning is thought to be rare, but plenty of people have seen it at very close quarters. It has been known, for example, to illuminate an unlit fluorescent light tube as it drifts underneath, presumably by inducing a charge into the atoms of gas inside.

The fact that Lucia Randles two experiences both happened on nights with much electricity in the air was noted by Jenny Randles when these tales were shared at Arrowe Park, just a few hundred yards from where they had occurred. Jenny privately speculated that somehow the static charge activated a sensitive area in Lucia's brain and allowed things to happen that normally lay dormant.

By chance, a violent electrical storm struck Arrowe Park during August 1984 while both Lucia and Jenny recovered from their respective operations. Right on cue Lucia had a further strange experience.

At 9am on 5 August, she greeted Jenny with the news, "My husband came to see me last night!" It soon became clear from her beaming smile that she did not mean that she had remarried. This visitor had been very much a supernormal one.

At 3am she had got out of bed feeling cold and donned her housecoat. Then that wonderful state of consciousness we call the Oz Factor took hold. Time stretched out, the ambient sounds found in all hospital wards (even at 3am) disappeared. Then he was there, standing in silhouette by the window and wearing a suit that he loved in life. He looked solid and yet was surrounded by a warm glow. Lucia was convinced that he had come to take her with him to the afterlife, but she said no, explaining she wanted to see her daughter have a child. Then he vanished.

Later, and against the odds given her advancing years, Lucia did beat the cancer that she had entered hospital to fight. Heaven, and seemingly her husband, was prepared to wait.

The view from above

Possibly there is something special about the site upon which Arrowe Park Hospital sits. Being surrounded by the strange mysteries of the Wirral it may be at a focal point of an energy field that circulates in this area. However, if so then this seems a beneficial, healing force and exactly the sort of unseen help a hospital could do with from the 'other side'.

While Jenny was in there for gall bladder surgery during August 1984 she discovered several other cases from patients and staff, though the medicos preferred not to talk about them too openly for fear of frightening those in their care. This was understandable but the professional attention offered was superb. If helpful energies are also concentrated here, they seem to help patients in their recovery rather than be terrifying.

One of the incidents that occurred in the wards that month involved James Aldridge who developed a sudden, allergic reaction to a drug injection. A lung became blocked and he started to suffocate. He experienced the wonderfully efficient and life saving actions of the nursing staff from a very unusual perspective. He saw it happen while floating above his bed!

James was suddenly propelled into this out of body state in an instant and, as it unfolded, all the pain and anxiety disappeared. He viewed the scene with a somewhat detached interest, as if he were watching a medical series on TV. James observed a patient in the next bed call for help and then saw a nurse rush over to begin the procedure to revive him. He described how he saw this as if looking through a gauze sheet, but with his mind clear and lucid. Then, suddenly, the patient was back in his bed, struggling to breathe, but on the road to recovery. The nurse confirmed later to Jenny Randles that his description matched what really occurred.

Out of body experiences (or OOBEs as they are called) are remarkably consistent and this account is typical of thousands on record. Jenny collected two more while on the wards and a nurse admitted that they received several reports from patients every year, but usually dismissed them as the result of hallucinations stimulated by the medications used. However, as Jenny explained, they are identical with many other cases where no drugs are taken, for example at the moment of a car accident. So this cannot be the whole solution. Something else must be going on.

Wallasey

At the very end of the M53 you arrive at Wallasey. To the south is Seacombe, with its ferry and the tunnel under the Mersey. To the north you arrive at Liscard and what comes closest to being called the centre of town. On the edge of Liscard, but heading south, is a church and just around the back from here a decidedly haunted house.

Daisy Jenkins, a lady of years more advanced than her features and vivaciousness suggested, lived here when we investigated the odd goings on. Some of them were very odd indeed.

They began when Daisy was young in 1903 and spanned the rest of the century. On that first occasion she was bouncing a ball against a wall in a timeless game that children still play. The ball fell into her hands and promptly dematerialised, never to be seen again.

However, other things were certainly seen again, including figures wandering around the house that only Daisy could perceive. It took a while for her to realise that these were ghosts because they looked like ordinary people, with the problem that to everybody else in the family they were utterly invisible.

Over the years, Daisy had many other experiences, including a vivid vision of a fire shortly before the tower ballroom at New Brighton was gutted, putting paid to the seaside resort's greatest landmark.

In 1969 her house was converted into three flats and one of her first lodgers was a man who lived alone. He became ill and during the illness the front doorbell kept ringing in the early hours of the morning. She suspected children playing pranks, but this seemed improbable night after night at between 3.00am and 5.00am! One night it went off incessantly (although nobody was ever there). The next morning the man unexpectedly died and the bell stopped working permanently. Daisy never fixed it and we assured ourselves that it was silent upon our visit.

However, a couple of days after this eerie experience Daisy saw a misty floating cloud in her kitchen. This gave off a sickly sweet smell and from out of it emerged the clear shape of the dead man. He then vanished, but she saw him again several other times.

This was followed by the invasion of the house by a mischievous poltergeist, which was plaguing her when we arrived.

Daisy drew £60 from the bank to pay a bill. She left it out ready for the morning, but when she came downstairs it had vanished. Months later it turned up again in a pile of junk that she had not touched since before drawing the cash out.

Other things kept vanishing and turning up in peculiar places. While we were there, she was on the hunt for the plug and flex attached to a reading lamp. The lamp was still where it had always been but the chord and plug had disappeared into limbo.

Also strange manifestations kept turning up on her carpet when she came down in the morning. Least annoying would be pools of water, which soon dried up, never leaving a stain. More troublesome were sprinklings of broken glass from no obvious source which could prove a real hazard.

The experiences continued for some years. They included strange patches of silver appearing in the garden and lights crawling up and down a brick wall at the back of the house.

Certainly, this building is one with a very interesting history.

Tunnel vision

The two Mersey tunnels carry thousands of people beneath the Mersey every hour from Wallasey and Birkenhead across to Liverpool. The oldest of these, Kingsway from Birkenhead, has a curious tale associated with it.

Shirley Tennant lived at the time at Newton, West Kirby, on the very edge of open land to the east on a modern estate. One day in June 1965 she was washing up the breakfast dishes at about 9.00am when something very odd took place.

Suddenly, what looked like a circular 'window' appeared ahead of her superimposed above the garden. It was fuzzy around the edges but displaying a clear image in the middle, almost like a colour TV (which in 1965 were uncommon in British homes).

Although Mrs Tennant could hear the normal background noises, the scene in her vision was like a silent movie. Action was unfolding but there was no sound associated with it. She was immersed in the activity taking place. It was as clear as day to her what was happening.

Shirley saw in this scene how her husband's car had run out of petrol in the middle of the tunnel. It was causing traffic chaos. In view of the serious hazard such stoppages pose, cars have to be towed away immediately and their owners are fined by patrols.

Mrs Tennant watched all of this taking place, including the payment of an amount that was the equivalent of £2.50, which was a considerable sum in those days. Then the image simply disappeared.

That evening when Mr Tennant arrived home she waited for him to say something, but he remained quite silent. He had, in fact, decided not to mention the incident because of his embarrassment. So Mrs Tennant asked why he had said nothing, before describing in full detail everything that had occurred, even giving him the correct time and the amount he had been fined.

Her husband was amazed, but soon insisted that she must have been picked up in another car and purposely tailed him into the tunnel, watching everything that occurred from behind. Shirley pointed out how ridiculous this was. She could not have known that something would go wrong.

Mr Tennant reminded his wife that the alternative explanation was just too incredible, but, unfortunately, Shirley Tennant explained, it was true.

Bidston Hill: A doorway to another world?

No look at the mysteries of the Wirral would be complete without a report on the bizarre track record of Bidston Hill, a recommended spot for walks or a picnic to simply gaze at the world. The only caution we offer is that, if some are to be believed, you may find yourself observing the events of more than one world passing by. You might also risk a close encounter with the unknown. For the hill seems to be a 'window' into another reality.

Bidston Hill is a small sandstone outcrop situated immediately east of the M53 as you approach junction 2. Wallasey is north, Birkenhead to the south and Moreton west. It stands out as a small island amid the tide of urbanisation washing all around it. On top is a windmill, some nice greenery with views over the flat Wirral landscape and an observatory and research station, where oceanographic, meteorological and astronomical studies have been made down the years. It has been considered 'special' by local people for centuries and even has some old rock carvings. Interestingly, it also has a sewage works opposite (another common denominator in reports of strange happenings).

Andy Roberts, a respected mystery hunter from Yorkshire, but one with a biting sense of humour, says he found (and reported in *UFO Brigantia*, issue 52) some interesting work he attributes to J R Kaighin in 1925. Kaighin looked into some strange events first reported nearly 100 years ago by an astronomer on the hill. These included slivers of silver that lit the sky and surrounding trees which also seemed to affect the instruments in the observatory, causing them to vibrate. Such effects are strikingly similar to those reported by the building contractors at Abney Hall in Cheadle, near another familiar sandstone outcrop full of strange phenomena. This must raise further suspicion of stresses and strains in the rocks triggering electrical activity into the surrounding atmosphere.

Indeed, the astronomer on Bidston Hill further spoke of strange sounds in the air, including low murmurs (possibly our old friend the hummadruzz again). He even stated that the series of events was " . . . as though some electric current, throbbing, palpitating, were at play . . . "

The scientist also noted mirage-like effects between the research site and the windmill, causing the air to be full of ghostly shapes superimposed on the hill slopes and described as " . . . thousands of glow worms, like a mighty host, had clambered up here . . . "

In more recent times a curious guardian seems to have stood by the hill as if nocturnally protecting the M53 and the housing estates around Upton.

A typical report came on 15 May 1980 from a local teacher, Gareth Hughes, returning home to Moreton at about 12.40am. The motorway was unusually quiet as he passed junction 3 and travelled towards the bridge that takes the road from Upton over toward its railway station on the other side of the carriageway. Immediately afterwards Mr Hughes would be preparing to leave the motorway, turning off to Moreton at junction 2.

However, to his right and slightly ahead was Bidston Hill and silhouetted against this, directly south of the weather station, was a dark, foreboding object. It was extremely large and close to the motorway, over the only open ground for some way either side, astride the railway station, which was, of course, closed at this hour of night.

At first it was the light that caught Gareth's attention, causing him to wonder why he had never spotted it before when driving past at night. As he passed under the bridge and wound down his window, he saw the object alongside him in all its glory. He slowed right down to a crawl as he went past the thing, which stood quite still, watching him like a police traffic patrol waiting for a driver to exceed the speed limit.

The black mass was so close and low down that it covered a substantial portion of the sky. It resembled two artillery shells placed side by side but angled downwards so that the front part pointed into the ground and the curved ends pointed skyward. The overall effect was not unlike a giant pair of binoculars trained onto the motorway.

From the front two beams of light, like headlamps, were shining towards the earth. They were strong but cut off sharply in mid-air before reaching the hillside. Two small red or pink flames also were visible at the back of the tubes, flickering slightly into the sky.

Gareth considered stopping, even though this is prohibited on British motorways. However, he then decided that he really needed another witness. The red flickers appeared at the back of the object, just like jet aircraft afterburners, while he was glancing forlornly around looking for other traffic. Had traffic been present, he would have seen it as he drove towards the massive object.

Mr Hughes continued, still travelling slowly, and glancing back at the slip-road to assure himself that the object was still visible. It had been there for about four minutes. He then went to his mother's house very close to the motorway, picked her up and drove back to the site. The object had completely disappeared, less than five minutes after last seeing it.

It is worth noting that at the time Jenny Randles was living less than a mile from Bidston Hill and was at home that night. She saw nothing, as did nobody else on the Wirral. Ironically she had passed the same spot under two hours earlier when returning home and been walking on Bidston Hill 48 hours before. If the object had been a helicopter, as some have speculated, there is little doubt that Jenny would have heard it, but, of course, she did not.

However, this incident was duplicated in most remarkable fashion on 27 December 1985 and this time there was more than just a single witness.

Nicola and Jack Limb, their young son, teenage daughter and her boyfriend were all returning to Wallasey late that evening after a trip to visit relatives in North Wales. They were on the M53 at exactly the same spot where, unknown to them, Gareth Hughes had been driving some five years before.

They observed the object hover directly over the same railway line at the foot of Bidston Hill, describing it as a triangle of lights, with two bright white ones at the front and a blob of red at the rear and top. Through the glare they were unable to see any shape behind the lights but did note that it wobbled or rocked from side to side. Again they slowed, hoping for other traffic. They too were surprised by the total lack of any other people or vehicles on the motorway. Again there was no sound coming from the object.

They kept the phenomenon in view until they passed junction 2. The motorway curves to the west and ends at the approach to Wallasey. The object was still hovering beneath the hill when they lost sight of it here.

Peter Hough discovered when he interviewed Nicola Limb that she had suffered for years from what she thought of as a curiosity. She kept hearing a drilling, humming, buzzing sound in the middle of the night, the source of which she could never identify. Once she woke Jack, and, although she could still hear it, he could not. This seems to be the hummadruzz making its presence felt yet again and it is intriguing that it seems to have an unexpected relationship with the odd goings on around Bidston Hill.

However, without doubt this next account was the weirdest of all reports connected with the hill, indeed probably with the entire Wirral itself. It was offered to Jenny by Bob Ramsey* from Rock Ferry, who contacted her in January 1983 after one of a series of broadcasts she was then making each week with Radio City in Liverpool.

Bob claimed that, when aged eight, a cloud of green mist formed in his bedroom and from this had materialised a gnome (remarkably like that in Bebbington just a couple of miles south). The gnome told Bob he did not belong on Earth, but somewhere else and proved itself by asking him to climb on a chair and find something on a cupboard top. As promised there was an empty bottle of whisky in a spot Bob could not have seen given his small stature.

Eventually, Bob started to see many strange lights over the Wirral and noted how these appeared to begin and end over Bidston Hill. He now received telepathic messages that this was because the Hill was a doorway that led directly through another dimension to the Pyrenees mountain range in Spain and another 'warp hole' under the North Sea. Out of this window emerged all sorts of strange entities coming onto Bidston Hill and he regularly went up there at night to confront them.

These entities were strange, ethereal forms, to which he gave odd names like 'the hairy pillar-boxes' to vaguely describe their appearance. They were engaged in an intergalactic war with Earth and its 'windows' as a prize. Bob was befriended by Algar, a more human looking alien scientist, whom others later met, including his wife. She confirmed this to us.

Once on the Mersey estuary Algar had materialised in front of a man walking by. He was so startled that he lost his hat in the wind out to sea! The silver disc in which Algar had arrived that day then flew south from near Wallasey town hall and hovered over Bob's house. It beamed a light down onto it. On arrival home he and Mrs Ramsey found that two spots of whiteness had appeared on their dirty carpet and over the next few hours these spread out and eventually left the entire floor space in pristine condition!

Sadly, Algar died in battle on 4 September 1981 and Bob nearly succumbed too, having to be rescued from the top of Bidston Hill, where strange shafts of light were shooting past (he called them laser beams). A group of semi-transparent, near invisible creatures like giant birds carried him down the slopes and away from the window to safety.

There is more to Bob's incredible tale, such as the aliens he met in the Tesco superstore in Birkenhead town centre, putting dozens of tins of dog food into a shopping trolley in an effort, he later discovered, to study Earth food! However, much of it is as hard to take in as is the bizarre idea that aliens run an extraterrestrial dry cleaning service.

Nevertheless, however you choose to regard this story, Bob Ramsey is certainly sincere. He has reported all these incidents to the Ministry of Defence, feeling this to be his duty, and we have confirmation of this from the MoD files in a letter dated two years after Jenny first interviewed him. Similarly, his wild stories look slightly less ridiculous given all the genuine and easier-to-believe happenings that have occurred around Bidston Hill down through the years. It is possible that the electric slivers of light and the rippling mirage-like forms allegedly seen by an astronomer on the hill decades ago could, today, be perceived quite differently. In our 'space age' society would they be seen as 'transparent aliens' firing 'laser beams' at one another?

As they say, one man's mirage is another man's close encounter. But which represents the 'real' truth about the uniqueness of this part of the Wirral?

All we can say for sure is that Bidston Hill is a very odd place and well worth a look on a dark, star-filled night when traffic is very quiet on the M53 motorway. Who knows what might be lurking in the shadows?

8

TOWARDS THE RIVER'S END

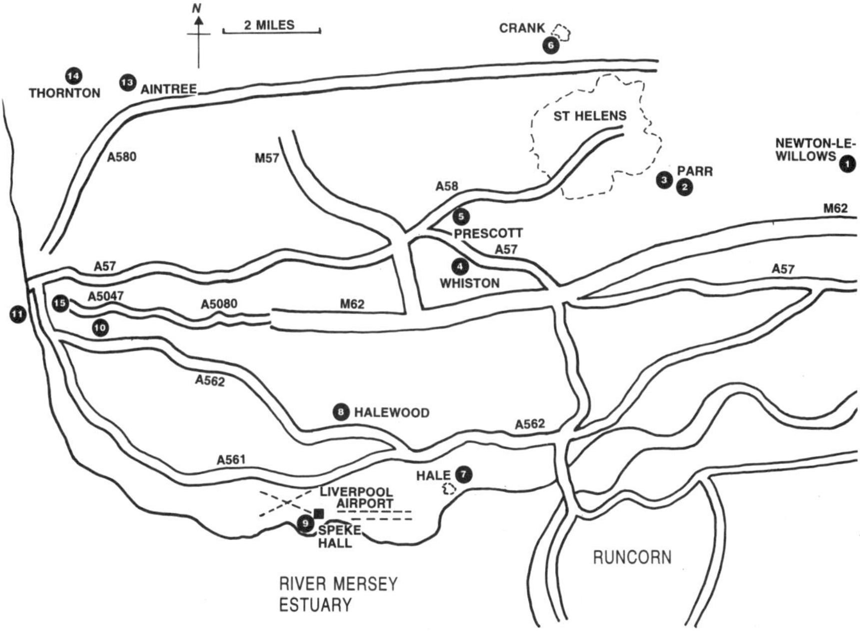

1.	Newton-le-Willows Phantom	2.	Parr Witchcraft
3.	Parr Ghost	4.	Whiston Ghost Sailor
5.	Prescott Road Poltergeist	6.	Crank Phantom Bunny
7.	Hale Giant	8.	Halewood Ball Lightning
9.	Speke Hall Ghost	10.	Penny Lane Poltergeist
11.	Ghost Sailor	12.	Seaforth Mermaid
13.	Aintree UFO	14.	Thornton Shroud
15.	Mermaid Theatre Warning		

The St Helens area and Liverpool

Looking down the Mersey estuary towards Liverpool, where stories of ghosts, mermaids and UFOs abound. (Peter Hough)

The white lady of Castle Hill

Castle Hill is in Newton-le-Willows near the boundary with Golborne. It is bordered on one side by a lake, and on the other by Newton Lane. The area has been spoilt by the intrusion of the M6 which scythes right across it.

Since the middle of the twentieth century an amorphous white figure has been seen in woods on the hill and along nearby roads. The apparition has earned the title of 'white lady', though some descriptions do not describe the appearance of a woman. Peter Hough heard of a local man who saw the ghost in the 1950s while poaching on Castle Hill. He described a white figure moving soundlessly towards him through the trees.

In the 1960s a cyclist was confronted by a huge figure taller than the average human being. The young man pedalled like fury until he reached the nearby East Lancashire Road. Another witness said he saw a motionless figure about six-feet tall and wearing a monk's habit with arms folded. Occasionally, the phenomenon has taken on a more aggressive role.

In 1970 a motorcyclist was travelling home from Golborne to Newton when a white figure drifted out in front of him. He felt an arm wrap itself around his neck and he was hurled from the machine. He abandoned the vehicle and would only return the following day with a police escort. A motorist described how the apparition had materialised in his headlights, causing him to swerve and crash the vehicle. Since the construction of the motorway there have been fewer sightings, although the 'white lady' was once seen floating across the carriageway.

Hell in St. Helens

The A572 takes the traveller from Newton-le-Willows to the St Helens district. East of St Helens is Parr and here one of the authors investigated a modern tale of witchcraft.

There are several examples in this book of how fear of The Unknown has driven people to violence. Indeed, it was fear of The Powers of Darkness which brought about the Witchcraft Act of 1736. It was under this act that nineteen witches were put to death at Lancaster Prison in August 1612. One of these was from St Helens. The Witchcraft Act was repealed in 1951, but as we know from the recent unfounded allegations of satanic ritual abuse and human sacrifice, the belief in witchcraft is still alive and kicking. Peter Hough interviewed one couple from Parr who told a story every bit as frightening as the latest plot from Merseyside horror writer Ramsey Campbell.

Colin Hale* spent eleven years in various covens. It started in the mid-sixties while he was an engineer working for a company affiliated to British Aerospace. A friend asked him if he would like to attend a meeting of people who discussed the occult. Colin was attracted by the idea, but did not realise he was being invited to attend the gathering of a local coven. By then he was hooked.

When the company moved him up to Manchester from Somerset, he joined one of four covens then operating in the area. What started out as mild curiosity had developed into a deep and secretive involvement. Before long he met a local girl and they married. He kept from her his witchcraft activities by a series of subterfuges.

"I had to work a lot of 'overtime', travel away 'on business', and when I ran out of those excuses, I simply knocked her out with a sleeping draught. It wasn't all spells; we used a lot of natural chemicals. Take 'magic mushrooms' for instance. They've been around for thousands of years, but they've just been re-discovered as a substitute for glue."

Eventually however, his secret life created an undercurrent which ended his marriage. At this time, he started work with another company based in St Helens. There, he became friendly with Pamela*, a Christian girl who was to become his second wife. Their relationship started with a bit of light bantering, then the occasional lunch together. Pamela was attracted to Colin, but she sensed there was something wrong about him. Then she had a nightmare.

In the dream she was in a graveyard situated near to the factory. As she stood by the edge of one particular grave, Colin suddenly rose from it like a vampire and stood on the edge next to her. Both stared at the writing on the headstone. As the images faded Pamela read the inscription carved into the stone.

The nightmare played on her mind, and the following lunch time she visited the grave yard with the Managing Director's secretary who was a close friend. The grave, including the inscription, was exactly as she had dreamt. Pamela had never set foot in there before. She met Colin and told him of the experience. Later, he decided to confess his background. Colin wondered what the significance of the dream might be, and he persuaded Pamela to help carry out some research on the grave.

It contained the remains of a man buried two hundred years before. Strangely, he had lived all his life in Knowsley, working on Lord Derby's estate. Why then had he been buried in St Helens? The couple discovered that, in the eighteenth century, anyone charged with practising witchcraft was denied burial in their own parish. Some old maps confirmed that in those days St Helens formed the parish boundary with Knowsley. Was the dream a warning to Pamela of Colin's active involvement with the occult? As their relationship deepened, Pamela was as determined to get Colin out as much as he was to get her into the coven.

In the midst of all this, the coven hierarchy promoted Colin to High Priest. Colin was convinced this was not a coincidence. The promotion meant he could form a coven of his own, providing he could find a Priestess, but Pamela would have none of it. Colin was now deeply in love with her. She used this as a lever, threatening to finish the relationship if he did not quit the coven. That was a watershed for Colin. Just as he decided to get out, the coven started working spells against the couple and things began to happen.

A voice which was neither male nor female and without age, spoke to Pamela on the telephone, delivering death threats. What followed were several near fatal car accidents. Once, Colin sensed a presence in the car with them, and he suddenly started choking as invisible hands squeezed around his neck. As the vehicle weaved dangerously about, Pamela started reciting the Lords Prayer, and the attack stopped.

Colin telephoned Pamela at work in a panic after a further attempt on his life. As they were talking, she noticed the figure of a man clothed in robes materialising in a corner of the deserted reception area. The figure crossed the room and began to strangle her. She managed to throw a switch on the switchboard which alerted the Managing Director's secretary. Pamela was discovered unconscious slumped across a chair on the far side of the room.

After this episode, Colin pleaded with the coven to let him go, but they told him he had to forget such 'nonsense'. Not long afterwards he awoke one morning with terrible stomach pains. As he drove to Pamela's mother's house they became worse by the minute. He arrived at 10am, and to this day has no conscious memory of what happened during the next nine hours.

Pamela told Peter Hough how Colin entered the house with the look of a mad man. She decided to get away from him and made the excuse she needed to buy some cigarettes. Colin offered to drive her to the shop and he was in no mood to be refused.

"At the junction with the main road, he stopped the car, even though the way was clear. He sat as if waiting for something. A lorry appeared, and as it drew closer he turned the car into it. I grabbed the wheel and averted a collision. By now I was hysterical, but all I could hear from him was how he had to kill me and kill himself."

Back home, Pamela persuaded her mother to leave the house and go across to a neighbour's. Colin followed Pamela into the garden and picked her up as if she was a rag doll, flinging her into a privet hedge. Fortunately she was only scratched. She ran after him into the house, foolishly hoping she could reason with the man. He laughed, and it was not his laugh, his face contorted and he came for her. She escaped outside, Colin stood in the doorway, screeching and laughing in that horrible voice.

In desperation Pamela cried out for God to help her. Immediately, Colin went as rigid as a board and fell forward, hitting his head with a loud smack on the concrete path. She turned him over, but miraculously there was not a mark on him. With the help of her mother who had reappeared after hearing all the noise, Colin was helped inside.

The young man had quietened down, but he was still not right. With his cooperation he was taken to some friends of Pamela's who telephoned the Reverend Ted Farmer* for help. Ted Farmer later told Peter Hough that, in his opinion, Colin was possessed by an evil spirit, and it was decided to carry out an exorcism. Colin kicked and thrashed about but the exorcism was successful. He felt as if he was re-born, as if a great weight had been taken off him. Yet he was still could not believe in God. When he confessed this to the Rev. Farmer, the vicar told him to ask God for a sign.

When the couple visited Warrington, they always took the same route through Winwick, past St Oswald's Church. They knew the story of the pig, and had often stopped to search for the carving in vain. After visiting the Reverend they continued to Warrington. As they came up to the traffic lights on the hill facing the church, Colin suddenly had an idea. He asked God to prove himself by showing them the pig.

"As we stopped, I looked up, and even though we were some distance away, I could see the pig as easily as if it was right in front of me. After parking the car, we went and took a closer look. It was eleven in the morning, and we just stood there like a couple of lunatics laughing and laughing."

The clown of Tickle Avenue

Years before Stephen King wrote his novel *IT* – the story of an ancient subterranean evil which took on the guise of a clown to ensnare its child victims, Stephanie Brown* and a friend had a peculiar experience which would have been at home in the book.

It took place in the early 1960s when Stephanie was about ten years old. She was with a group of other girls and they were playing down Tickle Avenue in Parr. One side of the avenue was a children's park, and opposite stood a row of terraced houses. The houses had been gutted and were awaiting demolition to make way for several shops. Typically of children, the girls preferred to play around the dangerous buildings than in the park.

They were outside the house next to the end of the row when Stephanie and a girl called Janice* peered through a broken window. They were looking into the front room of the house, when something made them gasp. Stephanie called the others over who gathered around eager to share in what had aroused their friends' interest, but they could not see anything. Stephanie and Janice could not understand why. It was as plain as day. Hanging in an alcove was a baggy clown costume. Janice suggested they went in to get it. The others stayed outside.

Inside the dilapidated house the walls were peeling and debris littered the floor. There was a strong smell of damp plaster and in places the floor boards had rotted. The girls giggled in the way children do when flirting with danger in places normally out of bounds to them. Stephanie and Janice paused in the doorway to the front room.

The room was black with mildew, yet in the midst of all the decay the costume hung there like a sparkling jewel. It was an incongruity. It was on a black hanger – a tomato red satin thing with white spots, frilly cuffs, ankles and collar. Suspended by a loop was a clown's hat with a white pom-pom sewn onto its apex. The girls looked at one another. Stephanie stepped over the threshold with Janice behind her.

This was no mean feat. It was like an obstacle course. The room was littered with rubbish and in places the floor had given way. Between them and the alcove was a gaping black hole.

The girls stood on the edge of the hole. Why could their friends not see the costume too? It was as vivid and real as their own Sunday School dresses hanging in the wardrobe. A rich, blood-red satin clown suit. They could easily reach out and touch it. Stephanie decided to do just that – she wanted to feel the fabric between her fingers.

"I reached out across the hole in the floor", Stephanie, now a mature woman, told Peter Hough. "All the while I was conscious of Janice standing just behind me. I stretched out my hand towards it, and as I did so, the costume *shimmered.*"

It was like the perfect reflection of a tree in a still pond suddenly disturbed by hundreds of tiny ripples. The effect frightened the girls. They turned and ran, oblivious to the dangers of the gutted house.

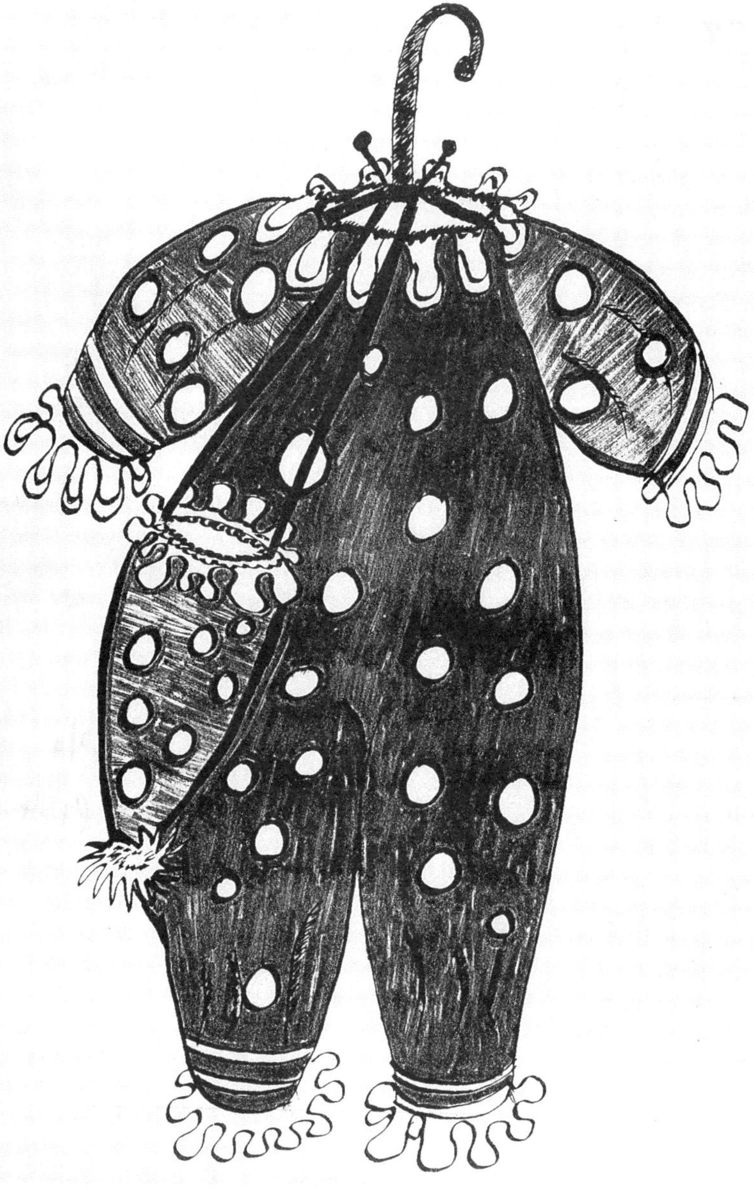

A drawing of the phantom clown costume by Stephanie Brown, who saw the object hanging in a derelict house on Tickle Avenue. (Peter Hough)

Just what was behind the experience? Why could Stephanie and her friend see the costume in such vivid reality, but the others could not? Was it the manifestation of an ancient evil living in the sewers beneath the St Helens streets, enticing young children with the jolly motif of the clown suit? Were Stephanie and Janice meant to fall through the hole in the floor? Stephen King – the truth might be stranger than your fiction!

Attempting to make sense of paranormal experiences is like living on the bottom of the ocean and trying to understand what submarines are and where they come from. The concept of 'land' would not even exist.

In this case, one of Stephanie's friends suggested that the experience could be connected with a little girl who had formerly lived in the house. Apparently she took part in many dancing contests, and it was thought that perhaps the costume had belonged to her. But why should it manifest itself in the gutted house, and to two children in particular?

Stephanie, who still lives in the Mersey Valley area, lost touch with Janice a long time ago. As a married woman she began collecting pot dolls of Pierrot, in traditional clown costume. She now has around thirty of the small sinister figures. When Peter pointed out the coincidence between her hobby and the bizarre childhood experience, it seemed to take her by surprise. She had never considered a connection, and her interest had begun when a friend gave her the first Pierrot doll.

Haunted St Helens

Nearby Whiston harbours the ghost of a sailor on Delph Lane. According to the story a couple had been out courting, and the young man – a seaman – saw his girlfriend home and bid her goodnight. He decided to take a short cut to his lodgings through a stone quarry. Unfortunately, in the dark he missed his footings and fell a hundred feet to his death. In 1945 a woman walking down Delph Lane saw a man on the footpath leading to the quarry. She came to within a few yards of him when he suddenly vanished.

Croppers Hill on Prescot Road was once called 'Combshop Brow' after a comb-maker who occupied a cottage on land nearby. At the bottom of Croppers Hill stood the Engineers' Hall. For many years, people claimed to have seen a ghostly figure peering through one of the windows, but events came to a head on Wednesday 24 September 1875.

At 3pm, a glass engraver was busy at work when he heard a shower of stones smashing through the front windows. Alerted by the noise the engraver looked out into the street and was astounded to see a large crowd of several hundred people. The factory boss went outside to find out what was going on. He was told that dozens of people had witnessed a phantom figure peering down at them through the front windows.

He pleaded with the crowd to leave, and when they refused he called the police who cleared them away. This did not stop the violence however. The windows were regularly broken, so the firm was forced to keep them permanently boarded up.

The phantom bunny of Crank

The aptly named village of Crank lies just north of St Helens on the B5201. It is notorious for several modern UFO encounters, but there is nothing to beat the story of the vengeful bunny!

It is set some time ago and concerns an old woman who lived in the village. She was an expert in herbal remedies and had a reputation as a healer. An obnoxious character called Pullen suffered from the 'wasting disease', so he went to the old woman for a cure. His condition worsened and Pullen concluded the woman was really a witch who had poisoned him.

Pullen got together with a poacher called Dick Piers, and they decided to destroy the old woman's power by bleeding her to death. They crept up to the cottage at night and broke in. The old woman was dragged from her bed and they set about cutting her arm. At that point, her granddaughter, Jenny, who was staying with her, came into the room carrying her pet rabbit.

Realising there was now a witness to their crime, the men chased Jenny out into the night. She escaped, but they found the rabbit which was kicked to death. The following day, Jenny's body was found by a farmer near Billinge Beacon. She had apparently fallen and died of her injuries.

This must had suited the murderers, but neither of them was to escape retribution. Dick Piers was the first to see the ghost of Jenny's rabbit. There was no mistaking the large floppy ears and great pink eyes. Whether it brought home to him the horror of the little girl's death is not known, but Piers went to a nearby quarry and threw himself off the rocky face.

Some time later Pullen was passing the now-deserted cottage and was suddenly confronted by the rabbit. Every time he moved, it moved too, in step-by-step imitation. The experience seems to have sent Pullen mad. He was discovered suffering from fright and exposure and was dead within a week.

As recently as the nineteenth century, the villagers of Crank and Rainford lived in fear of the phantom rabbit. It would jump out at travellers and hop alongside them. Several later died in mysterious circumstances. After a rail link with Rainford Junction was completed the sightings seemed to stop.

The Childe of Hale

The village of Hale covets a historical mystery. Situated between Widnes and Speke off the A562 the community lies close to the Mersey estuary at a point where it is three miles wide. The village pub is named after 'The Childe of Hale' whose remains rest in St Mary's churchyard.

John Middleton was born in 1578 and lived with his widowed mother in a thatched cottage. The boy was to grow into a giant, 9ft 3ins tall! He had to enter the building on hands and knees, and could only stand upright where the ceiling had been cut away. There is a tale of how he frightened off two burglars who thought they were pursued by the Devil.

When he was thirty-nine, Sir Gilbert Ireland of Hale Hall took the Childe down to London to challenge the King's champion. Sir Gilbert and his friends amused themselves by dressing him in luxurious clothes which were the fashion of the day. They adorned him with ruffs, striped doublet, embroidered girdle, plush breeches, green stockings, shoes with red heels and tie-ribbons and a sword hung on an embroidered shoulder belt. A plumed hat added to the spectacle of his enormous stature.

His encounter with the champion left the latter beaten with a dislocated thumb. This did not amuse James I, so John was paid twenty pounds and dismissed. On his return home he stayed at Brazenose College, Oxford, where his life-size portrait was painted. John then returned to the cottage where he had been born.

The cottage where John Middleton lived. The ceiling was removed to allow him to stand upright. (Peter Hough)

John Middleton died in 1623 and his remains were kept at Hale Hall for many years before being buried in the church graveyard. As time passed, many doubted the height of the Childe, and permission was granted for his remains to be exhumed. The thigh-bones were discovered to be as long as an average man's leg, and the hands 17ins from carpus to finger tip. Examination verified the height of 9ft 3ins.

The giant was a freak of nature, but legend adorned his growing with supernatural trappings. Some said it happened overnight due to a magical spell. Others claimed he had fallen asleep in a sandy hollow where he had become enchanted. He awoke to discover his clothes bursting apart as they failed to accommodate his rapidly expanding frame of bones and muscle. On his way home he tackled and defeated an angry bull. Folk lore painted a picture of a sixteenth century Incredible Hulk against a canvas of vivid reality.

The final resting place of 'The Childe of Hale' who died in 1623. (Peter Hough)

Four miles north of the village in Halewood, Jenny Randles heard of a modern mystery from a worker at the famous Ford factory. Billy was walking home towards Netherly at 9.30pm on a cold and overcast December night. It was the Friday before Christmas 1979. He was on a footpath in open country between two housing estates when he had a feeling that something was approaching him from behind.

"I felt a strange sensation down my back. The hair on my head and the back of my neck stood on end, and I was covered in goose pimples. I looked round and saw a white brightly-lit sphere."

Though there was no sound, Billy thought it was the headlight of an approaching motorbike, and moved aside to let it pass. But the light was a glowing ball about four feet in diameter.

"The object went past very quickly, about five feet off the ground. About twenty feet ahead of me it stopped, before shooting upwards at about forty-five degrees. Then, suddenly, it was gone. When I arrived home my hair was still standing on end!"

Did Billy witness the rare phenomenon of ball lightning, or was it an artificial device under intelligent control?

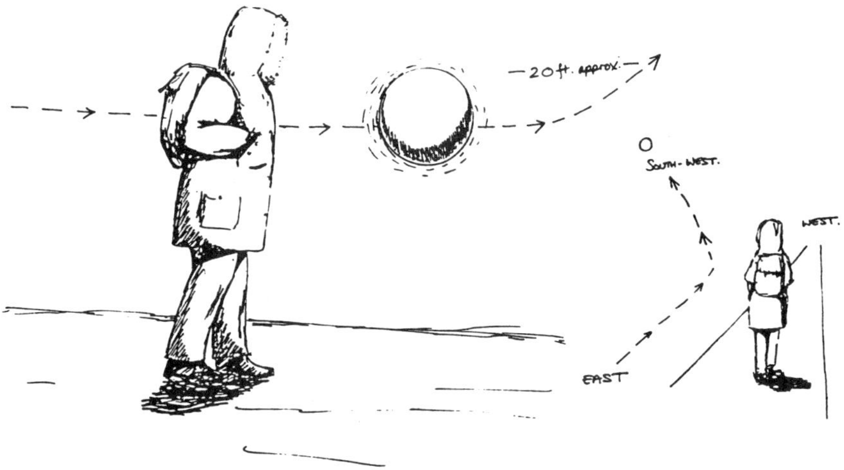

The drawing by 'Billy' of the strange ball of light that approached him during his walk home from work near Netherly.

Who or what was the sinister humanoid being who became lost in Wavertree one lunch time in 1976? The account was reported to Jenny Randles.

Mrs Lillian Davy was preparing a meal in her oven when she felt a presence behind her. She turned around and to her great surprise was confronted by a man at least six and a half foot in height. He had short blond hair and piercing blue eyes. Mrs Davy said he was very smartly dressed in a suit and shoes which seemed brand new. She asked him what he wanted, and he replied: "Have you any trousers?"

She said 'no', and he left by the kitchen door. As Mrs Davy looked out expecting to see the man go through the back gate she was bemused to find he had disappeared. An examination of the gate showed it was locked, and still puzzled she went out into the street looking for him. There was no sign.

Later she was describing the incident to a friend, when another neighbour approached in obvious distress. The young mother related how she had been making a bottle up for her baby in the kitchen. When this was done she walked into the living room to find the same smartly dressed man standing there!

He asked her for a glass of water, but she backed away and began to telephone for the police. While in the act she turned around to find the man had vanished just as quickly and quietly as he had appeared.

The ghost of Speke Hall

Speke Hall, just a quarter of a mile from the banks of the River Mersey and close to Liverpool Airport, dates originally from the fifteenth century. The black-and-white half-timbered house built around a square courtyard, once boasted a moat. The moat is long gone, but its ghost still lingers in the great hall, and labyrinth of corridors and rooms.

The sighting of a 'White Lady' has been linked to a previous occupant, although research into the story casts doubt on this historical supposition.

It was Sir William Norris who began construction of Speke Hall in 1490. A descendant of his – Mary Norris – inherited the hall in 1731. Five years later she married Lord Sidney Beauclerk, who by all accounts was a worthless being who enjoyed the high life at other people's expense. Just after the birth of his son, Lord Beauclerk returned to Speke from one of his gambling sprees in London. He confessed to Mary that his mounting debts had finally brought the family to ruin, and they faced certain poverty and disgrace.

According to tradition, in a moment of absolute despair, Mary threw her child out of the Tapestry Room window where he drowned in the moat, before fleeing into the great hall and taking her own life. It is said to be the anguished ghost of Mary Norris which has been recorded since the middle of the nineteenth century.

But how true is the historical connection? The tragic story is not supported by the facts. Lord Sidney Beauclerk died in 1744. His wife outlived him by twenty-two years – and their only child, Topham Beauclerk, survived to inherit the estate. Is the story a total fabrication, or did the tragedy really occur, but to someone else?

The Watt family who lived in the house from around 1795 until 1921 were sufficiently convinced of the story to get a large cradle which stands to this day in the Tapestry Room. Irrespective of the possible source of the haunting, there is little doubt of the phenomena itself, and many have seen the cradle rocked by invisible hands.

Mr P. W. G. Lawson, the Curator of the hall, told psychic investigator Peter Underwood that the Tapestry Room, built in 1598, has been the location for many sightings of the White Lady. It was Miss Adelaide Watt, the last private owner of Speke Hall, who watched the apparition disappear into the wall close to the window. Later investigation revealed the existence of a secret passage which led down into the grounds. In Tudor times there was a maze of priests' holes and escape tunnels in the fabric of the panelled walls. Sceptics have suggested that sightings of ghosts were really the clandestine movements of priests spotted using concealed doors.

The ghost is said to have appeared during a dinner party hosted by Miss Watt. Before it too disappeared into the wall, all the guests saw and spoke to it. Apart from the apparition, ghostly footsteps and disembodied voices have been heard in the rooms and corridors of this ancient building which sits on the banks of a much older river.

During mid June 1986, in Speke itself, mother and daughter Shirley and Elizabeth Kane received a shock in their council home when curtains began falling off their rails. Things hotted up with furniture, china, tins, an umbrella and even a television set being smashed against the walls.

Some neighbours became involved and were aghast at what they saw. Doug Holden told Peter Hough of how a hammer flew across a room and narrowly missed his head. Eventually, priest Father Paul Montgomery arrived. According to Mr Holden, the priest came to bless the house and say prayers. When he entered Elizabeth's room there was a loud crash. He came running downstairs, handed over the holy water exclaiming; "I'm off, it's beyond me!"

When interviewed, Father Montgomery stated: "I just don't know what has caused these strange events. The girl is about fourteen, and I've heard that strange things like this can happen to young women going through puberty – but I wouldn't like to use the word 'poltergeist' myself."

By the time the story came out in late July, the effects were already diminishing. Then an even uglier dimension took hold. In true medieval fashion, some of the Kane's neighbours decided the mother and daughter must be 'evil'. Consequently the house was stoned and several windows were broken. The family were given police protection to keep the mob at bay.

Liverpool legends

The mouth of the River Mersey finally disgorges its waters into the Irish Sea at Liverpool after a forty-mile journey, twisting and turning down through millions of years. Liverpool was a world-famous port long before the Mersey Beat of the 1960s. Yet the Beatles with 'Penny Lane', and the Gerry & The Pacemakers ode,'Ferry Across the Mersey', put the city on the world map for a new generation. Here, where the river is at its widest and most powerful, the area is rich in legend and mystery.

The Mersey itself has played its part. In the 18th century a smuggler was intercepted by Customs & Excise men while landing his cargo at Wallasey. He managed to escape and started rowing across the estuary but his boat was overwhelmed by a heavy tide and sunk. He managed to swim ashore at Liverpool where Customs officers caught up with him. The smuggler was kicked to death. Nearby on Leeds Street the David Lewis Northern Hospital was built. Over the years witnesses have described seeing a sailor wearing eighteenth century dress prowling the corridors.

The Castle de Burgh was demolished in Liverpool around the middle of the 19th century, putting an end to its ghostly reputation. The castle belonged to the de Burgh family, but in 1830 the last of the male line died. From then until its demolition, the castle was split up into apartments which were rented out. One tenant was a carpenter. Why he should become the focus of the ghost is not clear.

The haunting started – not in the castle itself – but several hundred yards away at the carpenter's work shop. He was working with four or five employees when they saw a gentleman dressed in mourning clothes walk past a bench. A terrible atmosphere filled the place. The carpenter broke out into a cold sweat, his body trembled violently and his hair stood on end. Suddenly every gas light in the work shop went out. The other men went home, and the carpenter decided to follow.

On arriving at the castle he heard footsteps behind. The carpenter turned, and saw the same man who had drifted through his work shop. He ran up the steps to his apartment, rushed inside, banged shut the door, then barred and bolted it. The carpenter leaned against the door with some relief, but this was short-lived. Standing before the fireplace was the man dressed in mourning clothes. The carpenter fainted.

The apparition was seen many times after that by other witnesses. A priest who came to the castle communed with the entity which told him it was 'not happy'. Was it the spirit of the last member of the de Burgh family, sad that the castle had been split up into apartments?

Dating from much earlier is the legend of the Mersey Mermaid. According to the story, a sailor returning from a long voyage saw a beautiful mermaid on Black Rock in the Mersey estuary. She was combing her long golden hair and the sailor pulled nearer the rocks to talk to her. He was immediately captivated by her beauty. She gave him a ring, promising that they would soon be reunited. Five days later the sailor died. Legend has it that his ghost appears on Black Rock warning other sailors to keep away.

Was this the same mermaid said to swim along an underground passage from the Mersey to Rostherne Mere every Easter Sunday? The story centred around some workmen hanging bells in Rostherne Church. One bell in particular kept rolling away from the church and into the mere. Finally, it was left in the water, and cursed by the workmen. The mermaid is said to ring the bell where it rests on the lake floor, then sit upon it singing.

According to a group of fisherman, there are stranger things in the Mersey than even mermaids.

Dave McCrimmon, a painter and decorator, liked to go sea-fishing in his spare time. He met up with a group of other men, and often took his sons, Carl who was ten, and thirteen-year old David. As he told Jenny Randles, there was one fishing trip he was never likely to forget!

It was a Saturday night in early May 1988 when the group set off into the estuary at Seaforth and stopped on some rocks to fish. The only light came from an unmanned lighthouse three miles away. It was a warm evening, and just after midnight when one of the men commented about a strange light in the sky. They all looked, and Dave saw in the northern sky a dazzling orange crescent shaped object, which reminded him of a banana!

The object descended until to the amazement of the fishermen it plunged into the water not far from the shore. Shock turned to fear as the first object was followed by a second, third, fourth, then finally a fifth which all disappeared beneath the Mersey.

The group speculated on what the objects – which were about the size of a car – might be. Ideas ranged from UFOs to secret military aircraft. They watched the water, filled with unease, when suddenly one of the objects emerged and flew off across the Irish Sea. They distinctly heard a humming sound similar to the drone of bees. One by one, the others re-appeared, following the flight of the first object.

Dave looked down at his sons and saw they were terrified. Carl, like several of the men, was visibly shaking. They decided to go home. Dave's wife suggested he call the police, but he decided this was a fisherman's story no one would believe!

The Penny Lane polt

Penny Lane, situated south of the city, is famous for more than just a song. The premises at number 44 were the location for spectacular poltergeist activity some years ago. Then, they were occupied by two printers who heard strange noises in the building, usually at weekends. There is no doubt the noises were unusual. During one weekend when the premises were empty, the sounds were so loud and violent that neighbours called the police, thinking vandals were ransacking the building. Trying to find an explanation, floor boards were removed and walls and furniture checked for mice and rats. Even after all this, noises were still heard and tape recorded, until, like most poltergeist activity, the phenomenon died a natural death.

Inmates of Liverpool Prison are haunted by a former prisoner residing in cell G2. William Kennedy was convicted of murdering an Essex police officer in 1927 and occupied G2 until his execution. Many prisoners have asked to move after awakening to find the figure of a man looming over them.

The Aintree thing

Over the years, the authors have investigated several fascinating UFO events near Liverpool. In 1984, Joe Le-Bôt owned and managed a model making shop in Aintree. He told Peter Hough of his first UFO sighting at Kirkdale, in the summer of 1974. On that occasion he was outside at around 11pm when he noticed a bright light travelling towards him across the Mersey from Wallasey. The light suddenly stopped directly above, and remained there for fifteen minutes, before suddenly taking off at speed.

Joe moved to Aintree and it was there, during the middle of September 1979, that he and his wife, Margaret, had the first of two strange experiences.

They lived in a flat above the shop. That evening, Margaret Le-Bôt's sister and two small children arrived to stay from the Midlands. Although the journey had been tiring, they stayed up chatting until 1am. Somewhere between 2am and 3am, the Le-Bôts were awoken by a bright light which lit their bedroom "like day". They went to the window and discovered that the entire area was lit up.

The couple crept into the lounge where their relatives were sleeping. That too was brightly lit. Through the lounge window they observed the surrounding buildings and sky awash with the strange light. It was as if something directly above the flat was shining down on them. Mr and Mrs Le-Bôt said it was tinged with blue, similar to ultraviolet light, or the light produced during arc welding.

It lasted for about an hour, sometimes growing dimmer then brightening again, until finally it went off, "like someone operating a switch". During this time the sister and her children remained fast asleep. The Le-Bôts were too afraid to venture outside. On the second occasion, it was a different matter.

Almost exactly three years later, Joe was disturbed by a flashing bright blue light. As before, the time was somewhere between 2am and 3am. Margaret joined him at the window. It was misty outside, but they could clearly make out a huge triangular wedge of light, shining down like a torch beam through smoke. Joe hastily dressed, and they stood outside, at the top of the wooden stairs that led down to the back street.

The silent wedge shaped light hung stationary in the sky for several minutes. It seemed to be a brightly lit object – and it was huge. This made nonsense to Joe Le-Bôt. He was familiar with aircraft – what they could and could not do. In his time Joe had flown many light aircraft, including Cessnas and Cherokees, plus a helicopter. This was doing the impossible.

Suddenly it began moving. Joe grabbed his zipper jacket and made his way down the stairs, through an entry and out onto the road at the front of the shop. As the object passed over travelling in the direction of Wallasey, it made a noise – a medium pitched growl.

The 'shroud' of Liverpool

The Turin Shroud was long believed to depict the crucified body of Christ, but in 1988 it was shown to be of Middle Ages origin. However, the formation of the negative image on the cloth remains problematic. Tests have shown that paints were not used, and scientists claimed it was not the result of chemicals or a freak medical condition. Now Liverpool had its own shroud mystery.

On 9 March 1981, a 44 year-old West Indian died in a hospice in Thornton. It was run by Hospice International – a non-denominational chain of hospices stretching across several continents. The man, known only as 'Les' was admitted eleven days earlier dying from a cancerous pancreas.

After his death the body was removed in the hospice bed sheet. Nurse Patricia Oliver disposed of the pajamas then started scrubbing the synthetic mattress with bleach. After several minutes work, she realised that the bleach was having no effect in removing a 'stain'. It was very peculiar, and she called over some other staff including Father Francis O'Leary, director of the hospice, and one of the founders of the organisation. They all stared in astonishment.

The stain was a detailed outline of the West Indian's body in its final pose. It showed the buttocks, upper legs, back, shoulders and the 'faintly visible shadow' of the twisted face. Clearest of all was the left arm on which Les had been lying. The image had been indelibly made on the mattress through pajamas and a sheet. None of the staff had ever come across anything like it before in many years of nursing the terminally ill.

Obvious parallels with the Turin Shroud must have been evident to those gathered around the mattress. Father O'Leary decided to lock it away in a cupboard, where it remained for five years. During that time the mystery nagged at him until he sought the advice of forensic scientists based in Liverpool. They came away baffled, and Father O'Leary next turned to the London Hospital Medical School.

It was here that Professor James Cameron had lectured on the forensic evidence that the Turin Shroud was the actual image of a crucified man. He is also famous for carrying out an autopsy on Rudolph Hess, and his work on Australia's 'Dingo Baby' case.

Cameron pointed out that the image on the Turin Shroud was produced where the body had been in contact with a cloth placed over it. In Liverpool the image represented the hollows created by the man's weight. He speculated that an alkaline fluid released from the body during the latter stages of pancreatic cancer might pool in these hollows. An enzymatic action might then transfer an image of the body to the plastic mattress.

The theory, which deserves serious consideration, was demonstrated during a television documentary. However, one wonders why there are no other known cases if the explanation is simply one of chemical reaction. And how could the fluid have been so evenly distributed to provide so much detail?

At the time of its discovery, staff speculated on the phenomenon being a religious miracle, and wondered on the man's sanctity. Little was known about Les beyond the fact he was a bachelor and had relatives in Bootle. Staff talked about him 'radiating an indefinable goodness', and said he was enthralled during the Mass held in the ward the night before he died.

There is one other mystery too. The logo of Hospice International, designed in 1970, features an open left hand with the thumb touching the upright of a cross. This is strangely similar to the outline of Les' hand where it meets the creases of the buttocks, themselves forming a cross of sorts.

The Mersey mystery mongers

This book would not be complete without mention of Merseyside's two most prolific fantasy and horror writers, Clive Barker and Ramsey Campbell. Both have produced best selling fiction and are internationally acclaimed. They broke the mould by using Liverpool as the setting for dozens of short stories and several novels, when it would have been commercially safer to place them in London or the United States. The people and dark sinister back streets of Liverpool are brought vividly to life by these two talented authors.

Clive Barker rose to fame with his best selling novel *Weave World*, and his collection of short stories published under the umbrella of *The Books of Blood*. *Weave World* is an ingenious story of a race of beings with supernatural powers reduced in size and encoded into the pattern of a carpet to escape destruction. The carpet is kept safe in a house in Liverpool, until it is time for the beings to resume their normal size to confront their enemy.

Ramsey Campbell was a prolific author while Clive Barker was still at school. Ramsey had his first collection of short stories published when he was only eighteen. Since then he has written well over two hundred stories and thirteen novels which include *The Parasite, Incarnate, The Hungry Moon, The Influence* and *Midnight Sun.* He is a devotee of American horror writer H. P. Lovecraft.

Lovecraft postulated another dimension populated by beings of enormous power. Most popular of these was 'Cthulhu'. The beings, who were banished from Earth for delving into black magic, occasionally reach through into our world creating supernatural evil. Campbell appreciates that the supernatural is more than a tool for imaginative fiction. Fantasy fiction merely explores questions and experiences that occur to us within the context of reality. He told Peter Hough:

"The Unknown can be something very beneficial, yet also seductive and dangerous. But that is the crux of all the striving for scientific knowledge – a journey out on to the fringes of the Unknown, grasping that shadowy something, struggling to make sense of it."

The Devil rides out

The Devil Rides Out was Dennis Wheàtley's occult best seller of the 1930s, still in print today. In it, a black magician called Mocata – based on real life occultist Alistair Crowley – pitches his powers against the Duke de Richelieu and his friends. It was made into a successful film, and on Thursday, 11 February 1993, it opened as a musical play at Liverpool's Neptune Theatre. Written by Colin McCourt, it starred Stuart Wolfenden, Bernadette Nolan, Karl Lornie, Gordon Kenny and Brett Forrest.

That first night began turbulently. It was the eve of the abduction and murder of three-year old James Bulger in Walton, and the sinking of a Haitian ferry aptly named The Neptune. Paranormal investigator Mark Glover heard of strange goings-on at the theatre and looked into the matter. The authors are grateful to him for information on the case.

Even before the opening night, Bernadette Nolan, of the Nolan Sisters singing group, had a strange experience. She was sitting at a bar in the Royal Institute on Colquitt Street, waiting to be interviewed by a journalist. She was completely alone for a while, but heard noises like someone working behind the bar – even though it was empty. She told

Did the Devil ride out to visit the Neptune Theatre in February 1993? (Mark Glover)

Mark that this was a new experience for her, and was not really a believer in 'ghosts'.

Mark interviewed many of the cast and staff and attended a performance of the play. During a recording made by Mark, anomalous voices appeared on the tape. Did the subject matter create an atmosphere of expectation where the most trivial of incidents was likely to be embellished with supernatural trappings? Or did the play open the gates to genuine occult manifestations?

Actors and staff said that the atmosphere in the theatre had been tense and uneasy all that day. Usherette Analesha Casells told Mark there was a feeling that something was 'not right about what they were doing'. That night and the one after, some actors and staff were frightened by fire doors opening and slamming shut of their own accord, and lighting equipment operating by itself. Lighting technician, Jackie Saunders, reported that she and her boyfriend had witnessed the fog machine start up spontaneously. This same machine went out of control on the last performance – Saturday, 20 February. David Hartley, of the stage management team, remarked that the theatre was much colder than is normally the case.

Gordon Kenny, one of the leading actors, felt unusually drained of energy, causing him to give a poor first night's performance. Others felt they were being watched. Director Brett Forest and another leading actor, claimed they saw a face in the technicians' gallery on the final night. The face was not familiar, and it vanished in a split second. Collette Croft, who is the stage manager, reported being touched by an invisible presence, and some actors had nightmares on the first night.

The phenomenon seems to have followed Jackie Saunders and her boyfriend home. As they approached their front door, both felt and heard a strange hard 'bump' against it. Jackie tried to sleep but suffered bad dreams, and dark marks appeared on her throat which faded by morning.

The theatre management told Mark that they were unaware of anything previous on the scale of the current crisis. However, it was reported, and confirmed by others, that the theatre was haunted by the apparition of one of the Crane brothers who built the theatre complex in the 1920s. The man hanged himself from the circle balcony, and people claim to have seen him walking in the aisles.

Analesha Casells thought the production's problems could have been related to the 'casting' on stage of a pentacle. A pentacle is a five-pointed star used by occultists to conjure up supernatural entities. Analesha, who is a white witch, said the pentacle should have been 'blessed' on the first night to block negative energies from entering the theatre. On her advice, this was done with salt water every other preceding night of the performance, and things became a lot better.

We have already cited hysteria as a possible explanation for the alleged happenings at The Neptune Theatre. Cynics might also suggest that the events were timely in creating publicity for the production, although Mark found no evidence of this. All the witnesses seemed genuinely sincere and obviously disturbed by the happenings.

Now we are at the end of our journey through the mysterious Mersey Valley, it would be apt to leave with a quote from the author of *The Devil Rides Out*, Dennis Wheatley, in his introduction to the novel:

"I feel it is only right to urge my readers, most strongly, to refrain from being drawn into the practice of the Secret Art. My own observations have led me to an absolute conviction that to do so would bring them into dangers of a very real and concrete nature."

In truth, many inhabitants of the Mersey Valley have become part of its magical legacy without seeking nor desiring its enchantments.

FURTHER READING

As active investigators and researchers of paranormal phenomena, much of the material in this book is the result of our own efforts, often based on first hand interviews and enquiries. However, we have listed the following publications which have assisted us in providing some background material. These may also help readers gain a broader perspective on cases that are discussed.

Alexander, Marc: *Haunted pubs in Britain and Ireland* (Sphere 1984)

Barnes, Wally: *Ghosts, Mysteries and Legends of Old Warrington* (Owl Books 1990)

Bord, Janet & Colin: *Sacred Waters* (Paladin 1986)

Bord, Janet & Colin: *Modern mysteries of Britain* (Grafton 1987)

Bord, Janet & Colin: *Atlas of Magical Britain* (Sidgwick & Jackson 1990)

Devereux, Paul: *Earthlights Revelation* (Cassell 1989)

Eyre, Kathleen: *Lancashire Legends* (Dalesman Books 1972)

Fishwick, Liet-Colonel, & Ditchfield, Rev P H: *Memorials of Old Lancashire* (Bemrose 1909)

Green, Andrew: *Our haunted kingdom* (Wolfe 1973)

Hough, Peter: *Witchcraft: A Strange Conflict* (Lutterworth 1991)

Hough, Peter & Randles, Jenny: *Looking For The Aliens* (Blandford 1992)

Oxley, C T: *The Haunted North Country* (self published booklet)

Randles, Jenny: *The Pennine UFO Mystery* (Grafton 1983)

Randles, Jenny: *Mind Monsters* (Aquarian 1990)

Randles, Jenny & Hough, Peter: *Scary Stories* (Futura 1991)

Randles, Jenny & Hough, Peter: *Spontaneous Human Combustion* (Hale 1992/Bantam 1993)

Suster, Gerald: *John Dee: Essential Readings* (Crucible 1986)

Underwood, Peter: *This Haunted Isle* (Javelin 1986)

Ward, Cyril: *Ghosts Of Leigh* (Leigh Local History Society booklet 1980)

Whittaker, Terance W: *Lancashire's Ghost & Legends* (Hale 1980)

Woods, Frederick: *Legends & Traditions of Cheshire* (Shiva 1983)

WHERE TO FIND OUT MORE

In general, if requesting assistance or expecting a response it always makes sense to include an SAE. All research into mysterious phenomena is carried out by unpaid people in their spare time and working for what are largely unfunded organisations. They do not have secretarial staff and big offices to handle what can be large amounts of mail, so please bear that in mind if you do not get an immediate reply.

Anomalies

Strange phenomena, from alien animals to time slips, are the province of two organisations, both with representatives in the region. The Society for Physical Research is primarily concerned with psychic phenomena (eg clairvoyance) and is much more focused around scientific and laboratory research. Their main London headquarters is a treasure trove of data and an easier access route is via their quarterly journal *Psi Researcher* which is a top notch review that debates current issues and brings latest news. ASSAP (the Association for Scientific Study of Anomalous Phenomena) is more readily accessible to general membership and investigates reports of almost anything strange. Peter Hough is a northern researcher who works with them and will be happy to forward details. *Fortean Times* is a news-stand magazine that has a witty style but reviews all that is odd and quirky across the anomaly field following the spirit of journalist Charles Fort. It's a terrific read.

ASSAP (Peter Hough), 6 Silsden Avenue, Lowton, Warrington WA3 1EN

Fortean Times, Box 2409, London NW5 4NP

PSI Researcher, c/o 20 Paul Street, Frome, Somerset BA11 1DX

Society for Psychical Research, 49 Marlows Road, London W8 6LA

Crop Circles

Crop circle research (sometimes called cereology) may be on the decline since two artists claimed to have faked hundreds of patterns. But the subject survives. In our view the best way to keep a weather-eye on the mystery is to follow the bi-monthly journal, *The Crop Watcher,* which remains, we think, the only one covering all aspects of the subject, from exposing hoaxers, to discussing theories and presenting site investigations. It regards itself as the 'Private Eye' of the crop circle world because it is unafraid to criticise anyone it feels deserves criticism and report inside stories often at some risk to its editor, Paul Fuller. Past issues have had detailed reports on north-west circles (eg at Preston Brook and Lower Peover).

The Crop Watcher, 3 Selbourne Court, Tavistock Close, Romsey SO51 7TY

UFOs

There are more UFO investigation societies than groups researching any other specialised anomaly. This can make it difficult to tell the good or bad from the merely indifferent. Some are strong supporters of the ETH (extra-terrestrial hypothesis) and convinced that the government hides the awesome truth about an alien invasion. Others are more wide-ranging in approach, taking on board everything from earthlights (ie forces triggered by the earth itself) to the overlap with psychic phenomena. NUFON (Northern UFO Network) is an informal liaison of the best dozen independent groups in the north and midlands, including MUFORA mentioned below. It was created in 1974 and produces a bi-monthly magazine, *Northern UFO News,* now one of the three or four oldest UFO journals in the world. It is a news orientated publication with precis reports of all UFO cases as they are investigated. In tandem with this is *UFO Brigantia,* a magazine format journal produced by the IUN group in Yorkshire, but more broadly relevant to the north. *Northern UFO News* and *Brigantia* operate a joint reduced price subscription package via either address.

MUFORA investigates UFO activity in the Mersey Valley area and also houses the Northern UFO Network files in central Manchester. These are accessible for research via prior appointment through

MUFORA address. About 2000 cases are located there, filed and dated for reference purposes. BUFORA (British UFO Research Association) is the main membership body, claiming nationally to be the oldest (founded 1962) and largest (many hundred of members). It has a British archives on computer of 15,000 cases, a trained investigation team, holds international conferences and issues many publications, including the bi-monthly *UFO Times* and more specialised reports. It brought out the first ever publication about crop circles (co-edited by Jenny Randles in 1986) and has offerings like the Vehicle Interference Catalogue referred to in this book. BUFORA also operates UFO-CALL, a premium charge line with weekly updated news and information reports offering a service about what is going on in both the UFO and (where relevant) the crop circle world. Jenny Randles has written and presented these messages since 1988.

BUFORA, Suite 1, 2C Leyton Road, Harpenden, Herts AL5 2TL

MUFORA, 6 Silsden Avenue, Lowton, Warrington WA3 1EN

Northern UFO News, 37 Heathbank Road, Stockport, Cheshire SK3 0UP

UFO Brigantia, 84 Elland Road, Brighouse, West Yorkshire HD6 2QR

UFO CALL, (Britain only - at premium rates, 36p per min off peak, 1993) 0898 121886

INDEX